The Illusion of Eve

The Illusion of Eve

Modern Woman's Quest for Identity

by Sidney Cornelia Callahan

«««« »»»»

SHEED AND WARD: NEW YORK

For my husband, Daniel,
and our children
Mark, Stephen, John, Peter, and Sarah

Contents

The Illusion of Eve

Is There a Problem?

There are some subjects which at certain moments in history need little introduction. Discussion and debate will have so crescendoed that the merest signal alerts everyone to the matter at hand. Today, the discussions on women have reached this advanced stage. Only the most complete isolation from all media of communication could keep someone unaware of the present turmoil. At every intellectual level the debate goes on. If one has no contact with professional journals, no matter; untold numbers of magazine articles have popularized their contents. The isolated magazine articles have been followed by whole issues devoted to reexamining the values, customs and facts involved in the current changes in women's lives. Such cover stories are followed by books, and then more and more books appear, some serious, some trivial and some merely sensational. Television programs and dramatic plays continue the theme, until finally, even popular Hollywood movies retail modern woman's traumas and conflicts.

What are these conflicts? What is the problem? Unfortunately, as in the case of most cultural crises, to define the problem is in itself the first major obstacle. As usual, there is even one extreme minority position that denies that there is any problem at all. These optimists maintain that modern women are wealthier, healthier, and happier than ever before. Polls are cited, statistics prepared to show that the vast majority of modern women are content; they and their sisters definitely repudiate the diagnosis and exhortations of a few fevered feminists who whine and rant about non-existent problems. Most women are affirming the traditional patterns of marriage and family life because it is to their advantage and happiness to do so. Families may move more, husbands help out more, and wives enrich themselves more in their increased leisure time, but the basic characteristics, work, and roles of the two sexes remain stable. One study of school children's response to questioning concluded, comfortingly, that if men from Mars should land, they could still distinguish men from women by their respective work roles. Confirmed spokesmen of the status quo minimize change and see women's major problem as avoiding the un-real world and exaggerated expectations of neurotic feminist agitators. Such outside agitators only create the seething discontented masses they supposedly describe.

At the other extreme, some observers estimate that one of the world's foremost modern problems is the suppression of women. Modern women are not only miserable, dis-traught, and deeply unhappy, but they are forced into neurotic defenses. The very worst bondage of all is "the housewife trap." Women in this intolerable situation may momentarily break down and run screaming through subur-ban streets. After, that is, they have exhausted the prevailing escapes into motherhood and/or affairs. Large families and rampant sexual immorality are proof enough of modern woman's neurotic lack of identity. Good relations with men are impossible, because true equality is denied. Men con-tribute to women's woe because they are seen as (a) castrated and enfeebled by domineering domestic shrews, or (b) mali-ciously maintaining themselves as a domineering, privileged and spoiled fraternity. Family life, social life, and the labor force suffer from the suppression of women. As for the seemingly contented men and women, the angry pessimists see their happiness as a sign of their lack of sensitive perception. Eventually, even the clods will be miserable. Modern women and their families are in deep trouble in a sick society.

Actually, neither extreme gloom nor extreme optimism is fully appropriate; reality lies somewhere in between. There are many more pressing worries in the world, but there are unavoidable problems and conflicts in modern women's situation which are not figments of feminine imagination. If only a minority are disturbed today, it is significant that it is the minority at the top: those women who are wealthy and well-educated and live in industrial, affluent societies. Unfortunately, problems (as with fashion and life-styles) permeate from a favored avant-garde to the encircling majority. When educated, wealthy women are dissatisfied with their traditional roles in society today, tomorrow the masses will be too. Change and communication are too rapid in our modern world for any group to long remain isolated. Once granted that there is a problem created by changing conditions and changing expectations, it follows that the problem will grow rather than diminish.

Since World War II the pace of life has quickened, marriage *has* changed, family life has changed, the old certainties of culture no longer convince automatically. The new problem of woman is, essentially, the nature of women and their role in a new society. Through no fault of their own, women have lost their roles and do not know where to find them. Imagine how few young women could duplicate their mother's life even if they wished to. There is an even greater distance and difference between a modern woman's world and her grandmother's situation. In the course of one or two generations three significant revolutionary developments have taken place affecting women: the legal and social emancipation of women, the advance in medical knowledge, and the progress of industrialization. These interrelated revolutions radically alter modern woman's situation and the decisions she must make.

The increasing numbers of employed women indicates one major change in custom and culture. In America, a 73 percent increase of employed women over the past ten years (to total over 9 million working women) reveals that today millions of families have either abandoned or found impossible the traditional pattern of family life. In these families father no longer supports the family alone while mother stays home, keeps the house, and raises the children. Admittedly, many of these working women reflect only the failure of the traditional pattern caused by the husband's death, divorce, or desertion. But many working women are from the high-income, well-educated families. They symbolize a new commitment to freely chosen work outside the home. Is this new pattern the result of the emancipation and education of women?

The emancipation of modern woman has followed the historical pattern of many another freedom movement. First the struggle for equality before the law is won and this legal advance (voting rights, adult status, right to own property, etc.) ameliorates blatant discrimination and injustices. This initial victory is then followed by a pause of exhaustion during which the original leaders of the cause fade away. (The early feminists seem a bit quaint and dated in their fervor, for who can even imagine denying women the right to vote or education?) But as the legal emancipation takes effect, a more educated and sophisticated generation of leaders arise with new demands. They push for full, final equality, a social emancipation with no compromises, evasions or reservations.

The privileged group (in this case, men) can no longer grant, condescendingly, concessions here and there; they simply must accept the new order and give up their former power and privilege. However, before that final day when the flag comes down, and the last club integrates, there occurs a phenomenon now widely known as "backlash." "The male backlash" has consisted of jokes, deprecating attitudes and more subtle discriminations. On analysis, it arises partly from the excesses of bitter feminists, partly from an alarm for the family structure, and partly from the wounded ego and pride of those who have heretofore ruled by divine right.

It is inevitable; when custom and a privileged caste lose control of a culture, there is a certain amount of confusion. Many who have been dominant are resentful, and many who have been comfortably suppressed are uneasy with their new freedom and responsibility. The stability of a society can waver while new values and new customs obtain their own equilibrium. Our present situation is one of women's reconstruction and new solutions. Before this, new freedom and equality had not as seriously disturbed the status quo, because equality was confined to single women or legal rights. But when the social equality of married women begins to be demanded, then the older patriarchal family life goes down. The traditional Western family structure is based upon masculine dominance and authority; it is naturally and logically incompatible with complete social equality and the emancipation of women.

Along with the emancipation of women there has come the amazing medical revolution which has reduced infant mortality, made childbearing safe and easy, and soon will produce a certain, safe, and acceptable control of fertility. These interrelated achievements radically alter women's life and the state of society. When most infants born live to adulthood, families and societies do not need as many births as formerly to maintain and increase their size. As families and populations become crowded, control of fertility can contribute to the common good. Parents are not only given a choice by the discovery of moral methods of family limitations, but in the present (and increasingly in the future) social indications and circumstances will justify smaller-sized families. Fewer births and excellent maternal care assure most modern women of more physical health and energy than women have ever known. Women's life expectancy has so risen that most women can look forward to twenty to thirty active, healthy years beyond menopause. It is not too much to say that modern women have been given a second life. Their childbearing years take a relatively short proportion of their life time and will not by any means wear them out.

Nor will woman's traditional work of maintaining food, clothing and shelter consume so much energy. The third great revolutionary change that affects women is the industrial society's mechanization of housekeeping. Modern plumbing, mass production of clothing and food, automated appliances, all have transformed traditional tasks. True, housekeeping standards have risen with the advent of machines. It is also true that appliances often barely equalize the increased work they impose; with washing machines and dryers one launders, with bathtubs one bathes, with vacuum cleaners one cleans, and so on. But with firm self-discipline affluent, automated housekeeping can be streamlined and compressed into a small portion of the day. If, that is, there are no children in the house. Industrialization may yet make

housework virtually automated, but childrearing in complicated industrial societies has become more arduous and
demanding than ever. Children not only require more food,
clothing, medicine, and medical care than before, but
require more time. Babies and small children must be supervised every minute to protect them from all the dangers of
a mechanized, urban environment. In addition, their cultural,
religious, and intellectual preparation must be complex,
intensive and extended before they can hope to take a
respected place in society. In a mobile society all of these
childrearing burdens fall upon the individual parents alone,
for they have probably left family far behind and cannot
afford hired help. Ironically, an extra burden lies in the fact
that the higher standard of childcare conflicts directly with
the increased housekeeping standards, so that an added
tension and conflict ensue.

Industrialization has created a paradox in modern woman's
situation. If there is nobody at home, there is not enough
hard, necessary housework to fill the days, but if there are
babies and small children in the family, there is an overwhelming amount of physical labor and psychological
pressure which the mother must bear in isolation. These
contradictory problems at different stages of woman's life
confuse the writing and advice given modern women. It is
ridiculous to tell an overworked young mother that modern
woman's problem arises from too much dissipated leisure.
Many a young mother may be near exhaustion every night
without having had any time to herself or having spent any
time or money for any luxuries. Yet women in a later stage
of life without the care of small children can feel that they
do not have enough demands upon them. These women and
their families do not have the money, space, health or energy

to cope with more children, but the mother may still have time, energy and talents that remain untapped.

It soon becomes clear in any discussion of modern women that numerous distinctions, and differences in age and stage of life must be taken into account. And more important, the differences between individuals and individual circumstances must be calculated. New freedom is in the end new opportunity for unique individual choice. But the more primary, and more interesting, problem is that of the principles which should govern the new decisions and choices. These guiding principles, whether acknowledged or not, will necessarily involve a prior choice of basic values and a particular view of mankind and the world. These more basic commitments and prior assumptions are the submerged portion of the iceberg labeled "modern woman's problems." These deeper problems are too often ignored in superficial discussions: the context of so many discussions is disappointingly limited, one-sided, and one-dimensional.

Committed Christians trying to integrate a new role for women within a Christian context are left amidst even greater confusions. The theological dimension of the woman question has had its own contradictions, missapprehensions and confining stereotypes. Perhaps the nadir of one Christian attitude can be seen in a certain prelate's advice to a group of Christian women concerned with social justice: those with grown families should "thank God for your period of inertia, stay home, perfect yourselves, and save your own souls."[1] The world of mistaken assumptions and bad theology behind these words needs to be demolished.

Unfortunately, before Christian women can progress they must pass through frail theological roadblocks and confront formidable barriers of culture and tradition. In the meleé popular cults here and there with their sentimental trappings and comforting rationalizations may have to be discarded, but in the long run more Christian freedom for women will impose more Christian responsibility, so neither the church nor society will suffer. Surely Christianity thrives upon the crashing of cultural idols, for the sacrifice of congenial fixations is the essence of all Christian growth. If Christians have been teaching a one-sided doctrine of woman's nature and woman's work, they must now restore the balance.

NOTES

[1] A. V. Krebs, Jr., "A Church of Silence," *The Commonweal,* LXXX (July 10, 1964), p. 472.

ONE

Two Different Solutions

When modern women are bombarded with directives and advice, they have good cause to feel confused. Not only are the directions for fulfilling their roles as women often contradictory, but, as often happens with directions, what is *not* said can cause trouble. One person's easy assumption may be another person's principal difficulty—and in discussing women, what seems an "obvious fact" to one may be neither "obvious" nor a "fact" to another. There are several basic and complex questions to be answered before recommending, for instance, that American women emulate Japanese women or campaign for Soviet-type childcare centers. Behind every recommendation are assumed answers to two basic questions: How different is woman from man? How important is this difference in the overall life and culture of mankind?

The second question obviously involves a choice of basic values; but the first, which might seem to be a scientific question, is hard to contain within a factual sphere. Physical and psychological differences between men and women could presumably be measured and recorded, but the subjective interpretation of the results makes their meaning debatable. One amusing example of this difficulty is the contradictory interpretation of the same empirical facts given by Simone de Beauvoir and Margaret Mead. The empirical datum in question is the biological difference in male and female physical sexual functions. This difference is bemoaned by an angry Miss de Beauvoir: poor women, they undergo the "curse" of debilitating menstruation, the hazards of childbirth after being drained by the unborn "parasite" within, and finally the uncertainties and catastrophes of menopause. No wonder man has enslaved this creature, already enslaved by her own physical processes. Man, on the other hand, has the advantage of a clear, consistent, free sexual development. Man has been free to do the really important things in the world; lucky, lucky men![1] But Margaret Mead couldn't disagree more thoroughly. She pities men, who, faced with the unsure onset of puberty, the unsure status of paternity, and the unsure end of potency, must compensate their insecurities by compensatory achievement. Women with their visible, immediate, productive, and defined sexual development have all the psychological advantage. Women are secure in their concrete creativity; fortunate women![2]

How differently are the same facts seen. Clearly, the different interpretations of male-female maturation were influenced by prior assumptions about the value of the body, the nature of creativity, and what is most important in a culture. In such an emotionally charged discussion almost every reading of the facts is colored by the individual's preconceived ideas and his cultural conditioning. But for all the individual shadings in these discussions, there is an overall pattern. Most writers on the woman question fall into one or the other school of thought. For the sake of clarity, I shall present the two schools of thought as though they were coherent, self-conscious parties. Of course, in the muddle of reality, there are no such tidy categories; for that matter, many writers are not even conscious of the assumptions underpinning their arguments. Still, in a survey of the literature two roughly opposite poles of thought can be observed.[3]

The first group of thinkers—I will call them "environmentalists"[4]—would take up de Beauvoir's assertion as a first principle: "One is not born, but becomes a woman."[5] In other words, there is very little essential, innate difference between men and women: culture and the environment produce the differences we observe. Attitudes, expectations, and conscious instruction from those around her, *teach* a woman how to be "feminine." Everyone and everything around her exert pressures upon a woman to behave and conform to the defined feminine role of her culture.

In our Western patriarchal culture, for instance, the feminine role has traditionally been that of the passive, emotional, intuitive, nurturing, loving wife and mother. Ambitious, abstract intellectual work and aggressive achievement in the world have been assigned to the male. This division of roles has been accompanied by a double standard of sexual behavior favoring masculine prerogatives. In fact, while stating their theoretical position, most thinkers of the environmentalist school become stridently indignant about the centuries of masculine exploitation of women. Women have been brutally denied their rights as full human persons! Their civil liberty has been denied them; opportunities for education have been denied them; employment and equal opportunity in the world of work have been denied them. They have been oppressed and degraded by a masculine culture that has treated them primarily as sexual objects, limited to pleasure and progeny.

This angry analysis of Western culture's suppression of women usually emphasizes woman's past bondage to her body. Unable to control fertility, women have been subjected to the debilitating effects of constant pregnancy and child-care. Condemned to constant sexual procreation, women have not had the physical energy or health to develop other aspects of their personalities. Furthermore, before indus-trialization the greater physical strength of men was always a factor in the subordination of women. In a crude culture the physically strong dominate the weak, and most women, being far less strong than men, have been at their mercy. Masculine oppressors might idealize and glorify woman's weakness as gentleness and grace, but underlying it all would be con-tempt and the power to subdue any woman not conforming to the submissive image.

In the patriarchal society, the pressure upon a woman to conform to the passive, subordinate, submissive role begins in infancy. Parents smile when little girls quietly play with dolls, and frown when they create with tools, or express un-seemly "masculine" ambitions. Education is thought of more as a social asset in marrying well than as a preparation for serious work. Beauty, charm and popularity count far more in the eyes of the family than do good grades and ability to work. The thesis clearly follows: if woman is told enough that her success in life depends upon success with men, she will soon believe it and lose confidence in her own powers.

The environmentalists further claim that man's exploita-tion of woman has been so complete that he and his culture have brainwashed woman into believing that she is happier in her exploited state. The white oppression of the Negro is pointed to as an example of a similar exploitation. The Negro too was made to conform to an image; he too was sup-posed to be passive, intuitive, emotionally happy; his safety and success with whites lay in playing his "Uncle Tom" role. But a new generation of Negroes in revolt against their sup-pression use "Uncle Tom" as an epithet denoting a contemptible, false conformity to the white man's expectations. Women also must be "Uncle Toms" in male cultures; many an example has been cited of college girls playing dumb on dates, business women forced to roundabout tactics, and career wives reduced to innumerable artifices. The general charge is that the despicable male ego is still dominant, still punishing women who threaten the supposed superiority of the masculine sex.

What is woman to do to achieve full recognition as an equal human person with the right of complete fulfillment? The environmentalist school, operating on the theory that culture has created the situation, asserts that culture can be changed for the better. Since the essential differences between men and women are held to be slight compared with those between members of the same sex or those imposed from without, the challenge is to change the customs and expectations of both men and women. Woman must disprove the stereotypes of inferiority by greater efforts at education and work in the world. She must be willing to make the sacrifices that will accompany and accomplish her coming to full freedom and responsibility in society. She must give up trying to please men and disregard masculine prejudices. Then, she must diligently apply herself to preparations for serious work in the world; to do this she must resist the current pressures for early marriage. When married, she must resist pressures for a large family; procreation must be carefully controlled to facilitate her education and career. One writer discussing this question deplored the fact that college women were indulging in "the luxury of large families" and choosing "biological creativity" instead of intellectual achievement. The trend toward large families among educated women is denounced as a return to the pre-contraceptive bondage of earlier times; having many children

is either a misguided indulgence in a feminine mystique or
a lazy escape from freedom, responsibility and intellectual
effort.

On the social level women must be given and must accept
a full share in society. They should be accorded equal education, equal pay and equal employment opportunities. As a
means to this end, women should demand and receive public
childcare centers, maternal leaves and other arrangements
allowing mothers to participate fully in the economy. Housework and confinement to the home are a waste of woman-
power and degrading to women (one writer compares the
home to a concentration camp). Inevitably, Russian women's
role in Communistic society is held up as a glowing example
of women's equality and fulfillment. The Russian childcare
centers are praised as a practical way to free mothers. The
kibbutz system in Israel is also praised as leading the way to
communal solutions for woman's freedom. Even the childrearing practices of primitive peoples are cited as examples
of ways in which a culture can free women for greater fulfillment. If prejudices, traditions and old taboos can be overcome, progress can and will come. It is only a matter of time.

To all of these ideas the opposing camp—I will call them
the "eternal feminine"—replies with resounding rebuttals.[6]
They maintain that women and men are very different indeed: the difference is innate, unchangeable and exceedingly
important. Women are physically, emotionally, and intellectually different from men and therefore should play a different role in society. Sex difference is such an innate and
essential factor in physique and personality that it is folly to
underestimate it. Not many of this school would completely
endorse Freud's statement that "anatomy is a woman's destiny," but physical and psychophysical factors are considered

a major element in woman's nature. They are fond of state-
ments like that of Alexis Carrel: "Take any cell from the
body and immediately the sex of the person can be determined. Men and women are different species of the human
race."[7]

Repeatedly, the manifold physical differences are catalogued: genitals, body hair, bone structure, metabolism, hormones, layers of body fat—even the different elbow hinges
that bar females from big-league baseball—all are brought
forward as evidence. Man's greater physical strength is heavily emphasized, while woman's ability to endure is stressed.
But, above all, the importance of procreative roles is re-
iterated. Childbirth is the highest physical fulfillment of a
woman's body: nothing is more important in her life. Instead
of the "bondage" and "drain" described by the cultural
school, pregnancy and childbirth are seen as physically beneficial to a woman's system and necessary to her physical maturity. The extra hormones present during pregnancy not
only enrich woman's health, but they also deeply affect her
emotional and mental attitudes.

The essence of psychic femininity, "the eternal feminine,"
is the psychological and emotional traits that accompany
motherhood. Women are physically equipped to carry and
nurture a child as no man can, and they are also psychologically equipped to love, protect, and nurture. They are
more concerned with "inner space" and have a different
concept of time. Woman by nature tends to inward passive-
receptive responses, while man is by nature the opposite.
Erich Fromm speaks for a whole group of writers in *The
Art of Loving* when he discusses sexual differences:

There is masculinity and femininity in *character* as well as in *sexual function*. The masculine character can be defined as having

the qualities of penetration, guidance, activity, discipline and adventurousness; the feminine character by the qualities of productive receptiveness, protection, realism, endurance, motherliness. (It must always be kept in mind that in each individual both characteristics are blended, but with the preponderance of those appertaining to "his" or "her" sex.)[8]

Fromm's parenthetical reservation is not always granted by some writers who see more than a "preponderance" of the differing qualities. The image most often used is that of opposing poles to describe the contrasting natures of men and women: all women who are "normal" will manifest feminine qualities and be highly unlike men. There is an intrinsic feminine norm of personality traits common to all women.

In the influential theory of "the feminine core," first proposed by the psychiatrist Helene Deutsch in *The Psychology of Women*,[9] less appealing qualities appear. The "feminine core" is not only described as productive receptivity, but also as a blend of narcissism, passivity, and masochism. Woman is this way because of the conflict-strewn path she must follow in her physical and psychic maturing. Many psychiatrists are sure that no woman can escape the psychological effects of penis envy, oedipal problems, the trauma of menstruation, and unstability of cyclical reproductive processes. Physically, woman must concentrate upon activity turned inward, and so, psychologically, she is determined to an intuitive-submissive role. Time and space will always be different for her, no matter what the culture attempts. Therefore, it is misguided to educate women for active, masculine, intellectual work—all intellectual training and work will endanger woman's femininity.

Femininity is woman's most precious commodity, certainly as valuable as masculine intellectual achievement. Woman, who in her monthly cycle reverberates with the phases of the moon, can through her intuitive kinship with nature mystically consecrate the world—especially in our age, so lacking in any primitive communion with creation. Woman's mission of restoring spiritual values and her ministry of "nurturing" are much more important than anything else she can do. As Lundberg and Farnham put it in *Woman, The Lost Sex*:

Nature permits men to create geometry, the calculus, poetry and music, but does not permit women to do so except spasmodically, having shaped them to other more decisive ends. Women's historic inability to distinguish themselves in objective creative work instead of being looked upon as a defect can be looked upon as a special virtue.[10]

"Nature" rather than culture is, then, *the* determining factor in femininity.

If some cultures have reversed the general sexual roles, they are simply the exceptions that prove the rule. Even many of the kibbutz women have returned to traditionally feminine work. By and large women everywhere and for all time have found fulfillment in a passive, nurturing role, centering in marriage and motherhood. As in the past, so in the future, science's control over procreation will prove to be mostly illusory and will certainly not plumb the depths of the feminine psyche. Woman will always basically fulfill herself in her husband, home and children. In doing so she will also preserve all the intangible but important values of Western culture.

The home and homemaking are glorified by these thinkers as the primary field of feminine work. If a woman must go into the world in an unfeminine role, she should try to create in the world the special feminine values of "nurturing." She

should never denature herself by imitating men or their exploitive, aggressive methods; the difference between the sexes
is a source of creativity in a culture and should be maintained. As Erich Fromm states it, "equality is bought at this
very price: women are equal because they are not different
any more. . . ."[11] Ideally, in the "eternal feminine" world
women and men should be equals at opposite poles of human
nature. Their sex roles should be clearly differentiated and
defined; women should be educated for a feminine life, not
educated as a man is educated. Proposals for "feminine" edu-
cations have ranged from banning feminine higher education, to college concentrations in homemaking, to higher
education centered on poetry and philosophy. At any rate, it
should be markedly different from a masculine, exploitive
education directed toward a career. Woman's place is in the
home, or if this is not possible, she must make the world a
home. If she is not physically a mother, then she must spiritually be a mother; woman can not deny her vocation, which is
to be the "heart" of the home and the world.

Naturally, the "eternal feminine" writers look with horror
upon Soviet woman and the Communist emphasis upon
equality and freedom for women. Instead of seeing the Soviet
woman working outside the home as an ideal, the Soviet
woman is the horrible example of woman robbed of her
highest role. Such economic exploitation of women not only
robs the child of home and mother, but results in a dull,
monotonous Communist culture where sex differences are
suppressed. In the end, women are no better off and Russia
remains a man's world. A more ideal feminine model would
be the Japanese or French woman who cultivates her feminine difference and special sexual role. Such women contribute beauty, creativity and stability to society. Women,

therefore, are more than foolish to sell their birthright for the mess of pottage labeled "equality" and "freedom."

The differences between the "environmentalist" and the "eternal feminine" schools are, then, substantial. Is it possible to conclude that one group of thinkers is right and one wrong? The question of whether femininity is innate and essential or only culturally determined is particularly puzzling. Does a woman *become* a woman, or is she born one? One reason this is so vexingly difficult to answer is because it is a smaller part of the larger problem: the mind-body relationship. The mystery of the relationship of the human mind to the human body is one of the most challenging frontiers of present-day scientific exploration. Since sexual differences involve both physical processes and mental attitudes, their interrelationships are still mainly in the region of the still-to-be-discovered. One does not have to be a scientist to see that each newly reported discovery or experiment upon this scientific frontier opens new vistas of complexity.

One dramatic contemporary development is the progress toward unraveling the mysteries of the genetic code and the functions of chromosomes. As if this were not enough, the discovery of a new, non-chromosomal process of heredity has been made. The main problem here for the discussion of women's nature is whether sex is a major or minor component in the overall scheme of heredity. What, for instance, is the significance of the fact that a form of mental retardation is the result of an abnormal sex chromosome, or that sexual mosaics are undeveloped? When news stories appear of reported sexual changes upon children, what has really been done? Unfortunately, the present pace of discovery is so great that it is impossible to evaluate fully new biological knowledge, much less contend with the larger implications for society.

The same complex vista holds when we question the effects of sexual hormones and the secondary characteristics they produce. The crucial question about hormones is how they work and whether they inevitably affect the mind and personality as well as determining beards, voice pitch, and reproduction cycles. Some researchers have claimed a correlation of high levels of fantasy with high levels of the feminine hormone, estrogen. If further studies find that certain mental states are inevitably caused by sexual hormones, then the argument for innate difference between the sexes would be strengthened. But how great the innate difference would be, would depend upon the proportionate difference in the hormone production of each man and each woman. In particular the question would arise of how determinative is woman's monthly production of the male hormone, androgen, and the effect upon men of their possession of the female hormone, estrogen. Perhaps further investigation of the experiments in which men are given female hormones to avoid heart attacks will elucidate the mysteries of hormonal effects. Are the men helped by some physical effect or by some change in emotional attitudes that relieves stress upon the functioning of their heart? Are there any harmful effects from injections of hormones of the opposite sex? Would men and women become more alike physically and mentally if given injections of the hormones of the opposite sex?

One more interesting and rarely discussed facet of the problem of sex differences is the fact that in certain races men and women are more physically alike than in others. Carleton S. Coon, in *The Origin of Races,* discusses sexual dimorphism, that is, the degree of differentiation between

adult males and females in a population. "Australian abo-
rigines and western Europeans," he says, "are highly variable;
Mongoloids little. As Tibetans dress and wear their hair
alike, it is sometimes difficult to tell whether any one person
is a man or a woman."[12] This is interesting in itself; but the
implications are even more so. Does the degree of physical
difference between men and women from race to race influence a culture's assignment of sexual roles? Where men and
women are more physically alike, are they thought to be
more psychologically alike? Or, for that matter, are they more
alike? Is the beardless Mongolian less different from his wife
than the hirsute Caucasian is from his? Is the greater similarity the result of heredity and/or hormone production? Do
the women produce more masculine hormones, or is their
variability in hormone production as great as women of
other races?

In discussions of Caucasian femininity, it is the variability
of the woman's cycle that is most often cited as the important
source of her emotional and psychological difference from
men. The variability and constant change in the body is
thought to ensure instability. Variability certainly exists during the childbearing years, but now that the life-span of the
average woman in the West is twenty years beyond menopause, a new feminine phase must be considered. What happens to the variable cycle of hormones after woman's change
of life? Is she then closer to man physically and psychologically? For that matter, does aging man also have a cycle of
hormone changes? In our culture it has often been noted
that age makes men and women more alike. Is this because
of hormonal changes, the demands of the culture, or a pattern of psychic development? One psychic interpretation of
growing similarity holds that with maturity, an individual

incorporates the characteristics of the other sex (*animus-anima*) that he or she heretofore repressed. But if this is so, which comes first, psychic development or hormones?

Again, there are at present no clear answers to these questions. But one thing is certain: the new explorations in psychosomatic medicine are bound to throw important light on the determination of femininity and the role of women. There is a growing realization of the mind's effect upon the body, for mental and emotional attitudes too often affect bodily development and functions. Psychosomatic medicine is no longer an unproved theory: there is a complex relationship between psyche and body. But how much of a relationship there is, and the exact mechanisms at work, still remain to be uncovered. Almost everyone, for example, grants that ulcers can have a psychic origin, but few would go so far as Georg Groddeck, a contemporary of Freud, who claimed to cure cancer by psychiatric treatment. Among other incredible things, he maintained that the psyche was so important that it could even determine height.[13] (His theory concerning height was that a child who could not face finding out about the sexuality of his parents would avoid grown-up knowledge by not growing *up*.) Such a theory is almost laughable, but upon second thought no more amazing than the fact that a child's growth can now be stimulated by injections of hormones.

Whether or not height is affected by the unconscious, it is almost certain that sexual functioning is. In women, mental and emotional attitudes affect menstruation, intercourse, childbirth and nursing. A strong aversion to nursing, for instance, can destroy one's milk supply; on the contrary, a strong motivation can enable a woman to nurse years after childbirth. As for childbirth itself, it is a well accepted fact that by mental, emotional, and physical conditioning it can sometimes be rendered painless. At the opposite extreme, Agnes de Mille reports that some female dancers dedicated to their careers have so suppressed their femininity that breast development is curtailed and menstruation ceases.[14] Moreover, there is a respectable theory that states that sterility (and miscarriage) is not always related to physical functioning, but can have psychological origins. Even more strange is Margaret Mead's assertion that psychologically induced sterility can affect a whole population. She postulates the theory that a native tribe can become extinct when faced with the white man not only because of physical causes such as disease, but because of some subtle psychological response which affects fertility and the tribe's birth rate.[15] Beyond all doubt, the mental and emotional attitudes of people affect their physical functioning.

Indeed, in exploring comparative attitudes and expressions of sexual differences among cultures, the environmentalist school effectively criticizes the "eternal feminine" theories. Followers of Freud and other defenders of the "anatomy is destiny" thesis of femininity do not usually credit the influence of the culture in which they live and analyze. The supposedly universal feminine mechanism of "penis envy" may occur only in societies where men are dominant and encouraged, and women are suppressed. "Womb envy" in little boys may be quite likely in matriarchal cultures. Even the "feminine core" theory, with women condemned to innate passivity, masochism and narcissism, can be discredited when it is pointed out that it is based upon research with American women in Boston clinics. Neither the Irish nor the Yankees are noted for their balanced sexuality. It is never safe, fortunately, to generalize from the traumas of Boston; after all, in some tribes and other cultures menstruation is not a traumatic curse, but rather cause for celebration and the conferring of privileges.

The general attitude of society toward sexuality and the previous cultural conditioning does make, therefore, an enormous difference.

In the end, although neither side can yet prove a case for innate femininity or conditioned femininity, the case for cultural conditioning seems stronger. When confronted with the wide range of individual differences within a sex, and the very different cultural patterns existent, the biological basis of sexual differences seems relatively less determinative. As the social sciences progress and investigate the formation of individual personality, they find that the influence and expectations of the family and the culture operate early. Physical *mal*-functioning can wreck personalities and societies (plague, brain tumors), but in man's positive development, mental and social processes are decisive. When, for instance, cultural and physical conditioning can produce painless childbirth, it becomes evident that the brain's capacity for the selection and interpretation of physical stimuli is far more powerful than previously acknowledged. The tests which are supposed to prove the contrary are unsatisfactory because the subjects, and devisors of the test, are already conditioned by a masculine dominated society. Experiments like Erik Erikson's in which boys built towers with their therapeutic play equipment and girls built enclosures do not conclusively prove an innate sexual difference in perceiving space and time.[16] For one thing the children were too old; but more significantly, in the same experiment a Negro boy built his tower *under* the table. This response could indicate a socially conditioned different response far more drastic than towers versus enclosures.

Conditioning versus innate difference is still an insoluble problem, but when forced to choose the evidence seems to support the contention that, for the most part, "one becomes a woman." There is always the possibility that some new discovery may modify the argument; but in that unlikely event, it is more than likely that the research necessary to find the innate sexual difference will lead to artificial control. The knowledge and understanding of ovulation, for instance, has been followed by man's ability to suppress it. As man stands upon the threshold of what has been termed the biological revolution, the control of life, it seems a likely prospect that all sexual differences might be rationally controlled. But with the rational control of life would come new problems, as with the discovery of atomic energy. Man's challenge shifts from obtaining new knowledge and control to the right use of his new powers.

So let us assume that the future will bring increasing control over every facet of sexuality: sexual development, reproduction, hormone production, psychological attitudes, cultural conditioning. The problem of women would then become what woman ought to be, in herself, in relation to man, and to society as a whole. Should women cultivate and accentuate differences from men, or should they strive for identity in all but reproductive roles? Are differences in sexual roles essential in the rearing of children and in maintaining stability in society? The scientific questions can pale before the question of which values should govern woman's development. I suggest that it is this conflict of values that is really being fought over today. The two opposing party lines presented earlier are actually trying to convince women of what they should be. Is it possible to make a preliminary choice between the values each endorses for women, even before a more detailed discussion and examination?

Certainly, the values stressed by the "environmentalist" school seem attractive. Yes, every individual human person, regardless of sex, should develop to his or her full potential. Granted, there should be none of the past discrimination against women; society should provide equal education, and equal opportunities for women to use all their talents in useful, productive work. Women should not be arbitrarily confined to domestic work in the home or stereotyped feminine work in the world. The individual's freedom, dignity and specific talents should come before sexual identity.

Yes, also, to the environmentalist's stress upon accepting man's control of the world. It is good to develop the science and technology which will free woman from domestic drudgery, improve maternal health, and provide work outside the home for women. It is important to accept all that is positive in our present culture and not condemn developments because they are new and different. And so, finally, a yes to the insights and perspectives gained from comparing our cultural assumptions with those of other people. Such an attempt to free ideas of femininity from particular cultural prejudices and concentrate upon future development is of great value.

But then there are less attractive aspects to the proposals of this group for women. A certain Manichean odor arises from talk of woman's enslavement to her body and sexual functioning. At what point does projected control of nature shade into a rejection of the body and physical processes? Control can become abuse; and as a general rule this school assumes artificial contraceptives, does not balk at abortion, and repudiates Christian ideas of marriage and parenthood as outmoded. Few would go so far as Simone de Beauvoir in repealing marriage and recommending male brothels for ladies to patronize, but her proposals point out that equality with men only leads to the next problem, equality with men for what? Indeed, the aggressive attitude toward men is distressing; men are too often pictured as oppressive brutes.

The problem of woman's role soon expands to the problem of man and woman's role. For one thing, an unqualified, uncritical acceptance of the "masculine" values of our culture is suspect. Are the equal work of women and equal opportunities only to be for the sake of exploiting others and aggressively achieving selfish ends? No wonder there is a contempt for all "stupid" manual work, especially unpaid (unselfish?) domestic work in the home. For this group the only work that counts is that intellectual, professional work which our society rewards with status and financial emoluments. Ultimately, the "worthwhile" is determined by the society.

Unfortunately, too, the work of childraising is dangerously minimized. It is too readily assumed that mother substitutes or communal nurseries could free the mother for "meaningful" work. But can a communal nursery raise children well? Perhaps in our pluralistic, mobile, individualistic society, a child needs more individual care than ever to obtain emotional security, to say nothing of moral and cultural values. The personal fulfillment of the mother, or even the other needs of society cannot infringe on the personal fulfillment of the child.

With such reservations about the cultural school, one is ready to accept enthusiastically certain values of the champions of traditional femininity. Yes, to the eternal feminine school's stress upon the importance of the mother to the child. Yes, also, to cultivating aesthetic, spiritual, and ethical values in the home. Yes, again, to the happy acceptance of reproductive differences between men and women with its high valuation of sexual functioning and physical creativity. The body, the physical world, matter in all forms is well esteemed, and housework and the domestic arts can be a celebration of nature. The contemplative and charitable aspect of manual labor is appreciated. It *is* important that women should be prepared for this side of life and value it highly. The true values of life do not necessarily coincide with the values society rewards with money and status. Love, the gift of self, and the hidden contemplative aspect of the traditional feminine role are important and not to be dismissed. The development of psychiatry alone has shown the importance of these intangibles in the human person's development.

But one demurs when this view is carried too far. Irrationality cannot pass for mysticism. Glorious verbal assertions of what is feminine do not always correlate with reality. A woman is more than a sexual being; to deny her active intellectual powers expression is discrimination based on an inadequate scientific theory. It has not been proved that there is such a thing as a "feminine core," and it is rash to assert that intellectual training diminishes femininity. Women's education and opportunities should not be curtailed because of an unproved theory that her intelligence is different from man's. When the difference between men and women is overemphasized, the corollary is always discrimination in the guise of an irrational mysticism of sacrifice. Women are often denied equal rights and opportunity because it is said that her true fulfillment (determined by men and suspiciously convenient) is in giving herself to her husband, children and her home.

The overemphasis upon sex and the physical differences is accompanied also by an overemphasis upon housekeeping. The cult of breadbaking and other domestic arts flourishes as appropriately feminine. What begins as a restoration and celebration of matter becomes a tyranny of things. Moreover, it is often a manifestation of nostalgia for a bygone rural culture, rather than a rational response to present-day life. If the cultural school has taints of gnosticism, the conservative traditional approach to femininity brings to mind the pervasive influence of the Mother Goddess of antiquity with her nature and fertility cults. The "fertility cult" requirement that every woman must find fulfillment only in husband and large family is unbalanced.

At this point, after a cursory criticism of the two opposing poles of thought on women, it becomes clear that Christian values both confirm and collide with parts of both solutions. A Christian synthesis of the best of both arguments is badly needed. But before that can be done, a Christian view of woman has to be determined. This is no easy task, for conflicts within Christianity over the role of woman have never quite been stilled. Today as revolutionary winds blow within the Church, traditional ideas about women must be re-examined.

NOTES

[1] Simone de Beauvoir, *The Second Sex* (New York: Bantam Books, 1961), pp. 23 ff.

[2] Margaret Mead, *Male and Female* (New York: Morrow, 1949), p. 81.

[3] Cf. Dan Sullivan, "Why There Never Was a Great Woman Philosopher," *Review of Metaphysics*, (June, 1962), p. 559; Dorothy Dohen, *Women in Wonderland* (New York: Sheed & Ward, 1960), esp. chapter 3; and also the contrast between articles in *American Women: The Changing Image*, ed. Beverly B. Cassara (Boston: Beacon Press, 1962).

[4] Cf. Simone de Beauvoir, Betty Friedan, Mira Komarovsky, Karen Horney, Marya Mannes, Alice Rossi, and sometimes Margaret Mead.

[5] Simone de Beauvoir, *op. cit.*, p. 249.

[6] Cf. Sigmund Freud, Helene Deutsch, Erich Fromm, Theodore Reik, Lundberg and Farnham, Lynn White, Erik Erikson, Esther

Matthews, Lucius Cervantes, Gertrude von Le Fort and Phyllis McGinley.

[7] Lucius Cervantes, *And God Made Them Man and Woman* (Chicago: Regnery, 1959), p. 19.

[8] Erich Fromm, *The Art of Loving* (New York: Harper, 1956), p. 39.

[9] Helene Deutsch, *The Psychology of Women: A Psychoanalytic Interpretation* (New York: Grune and Stratton, 1944), Vol. I and II.

[10] Marynia Farnham and Ferdinand Lundberg, *Modern Women: The Lost Sex* (New York: Harper, 1947), Appendix, p. 384.

[11] Erich Fromm, *op. cit.*, p. 15.

[12] Carleton S. Coon, *The Origin of Races* (New York: Knopf, 1962), p. 27.

[13] Georg Groddeck, *The Book of the It* (New York: Vintage Books, 1961).

[14] Agnes de Mille, "The Milk of Paradise," in *American Women: The Changing Image,* ed. by Beverly B. Cassara, *op. cit.*, p. 135.

[15] *Male and Female, op. cit.*, pp. 225, 238.

[16] Erik Erikson, *Childhood and Society*, 2d. ed. (New York: W. W. Norton, 1963), p. 103.

TWO »»»

Christian Woman in Scripture

In searching for a Christian approach to woman, it is only natural to turn first to God's Word found in Scripture. But in the complex collection of books that make up the Bible, there are innumerable references to women. Which passages should be discussed? My principle of selection will be to re-examine the frequently quoted texts, but also, and no less importantly, to discuss relevant passages which are frequently overlooked. In a balanced discussion difficulties have to be faced; it is unconvincing simply to ignore texts that offend the current ideas. Such methods were certainly used in the past: some interpreters managed to overlook those passages which present a positive image of woman and propounded a pessimistic view based on "hard" anti-feminine passages. The result was often enough a distortion; and a distortion, unfortunately, which many found persuasive.

How was this possible? A model for use in constructing an anti-feminine biblical message is easy enough to fashion. The first axiom is that all women everywhere share the mindlessness and weakness of Eve, as well as her greater guilt in the fall of man. Woman, "the weaker vessel," had and still has a special propensity for sin. As the Epistle to Timothy puts it, women are to be submissive because "Adam was not deceived, but the woman was deceived and was in sin" (1 Timothy 2:14). But even before the Fall, the hier-

archy of things had been established: God is to man as man
is to woman. The man is "the head of woman," for man "is
the image and glory of God" while woman "is the glory of
man" (1 Cor. 11:7). It is only fitting that woman be submissive to man since in the very beginning "man was not
created for woman, but woman for man" (1 Cor. 11:8).

Moreover, all Christian women are urged to be "subject to
their husbands" as to the Lord. They are instructed to be
obedient, domestic and chaste. Above all, they are to be
quiet: "For I do not allow a woman to teach, or to exercise
authority over men; but she is to keep quiet" (1 Tim. 2:12).
Again, women are forbidden to speak in church; they
are to "learn in silence with all submission . . . if they wish
to learn anything let them ask their husbands at home"
(1 Cor. 14:35). "A quiet and gentle spirit," St. Peter emphasizes, is fitting in women (1 Peter 3:5); wives should look to
the obedience of Sara to Abraham as an example. But what
then are women to do? Their one hope of redeeming Eve's
sin is prescribed in 1 Timothy: "Yet women will be saved
by childbearing . . ." (2:13).

Need we go any further? If one took into account only
these texts, it would appear that the New Testament gives
divine approval to the old maxim that "It is, always has been,
and always will be a man's world." Worse still, they seem to
give ample support to Simone de Beauvoir's harsh accusation
that Christianity has "contributed no little to the oppression
of women."

But there is far more to the biblical view of women than
these few texts taken in isolation would suggest. Regrettably,
however, these are the texts which are most noticed; they
have obscured another side of the biblical whole which is no
less important. Christianity is a revolutionary religion; its
view of woman is a part of that revolution. Christ came and

made all things new. By His coming all values and relation-ships were changed. All men—and all women—would now be measured by the way in which they followed Christ and lived by His teachings. The judgment of the world became un-important, as did the external differences between one human being and another. Union with Christ implied a union of one person with another that superseded all other divisions.

As St. Paul says in his letter to the Galatians: "For all you who have been baptized in Christ, have put on Christ. There is neither Jew nor Greek; there is neither slave nor freeman; there is neither male nor female. For you are all one in Christ Jesus" (Gal. 4:27-28). It is, then, not race or civil sta-tus or sex which is important, but our corporate "life in the Lord." It is the response of the individual to Christ which makes him a participant in the new order; it is that and not a person's sex which counts. Christ seems to make this point all the more explicit when, in answer to his mother and brethren's summons, he looked "round on those who were sitting about Him" and said, "Behold my mother and my brethren. For whoever does the will of God, he is my brother and sister and mother" (Mark 3:34-35). Sexual identity, family relationships—all are transcended by "whoever does the will of God." Women therefore are also called.

Christ Himself treated women with a revolutionary equal-ity—and thereby constantly shocked the masculine prejudices of His disciples: "They wondered that He spoke with a woman." Christ never referred to woman as a daughter of Eve in her guilt; nor did He pronounce her to belong to the weaker sex. Instead He taught women, healed women, for-gave them, and cherished them as friends: "He loved Mary and Martha of Bethany"; and certainly Mary Magdelene, "from whom seven devils had gone out," was close to Christ. The Magdelene along with "Joanna, the wife of Chuza,

Herod's steward, and Suzanna, and many others," travelled
with Jesus and the twelve as He preached the good news of
the kingdom. Women accompanied Christ on His preaching
and healing journeys. They accompanied Him to Calvary.
Faithful in death, women were the first to meet the Resurrected One. From the very beginning to the very end the
good news was shared by women.

Women continued to take a prominent place in the early
Church. It is almost certain that they were full participants
at Pentecost. In the Acts of the Apostles, the description of
those present names the Apostles, and concludes by saying
that "All those with one mind continued steadfastly in
prayer with the women and Mary, the mother of Jesus, and
with his brethren" (Acts 1:14). Who were these "women"?
They were most probably the same women who had followed
and served the Lord. Is it likely that the women were excluded when "they were all together in one place" and were
"all filled with the Holy Spirit" (Acts 2:4). Peter, in his
great Pentecostal sermon, certainly indicates that women
were participants. He explains what has happened as the fulfillment of the prophecy of Joel. The Lord has poured forth
His Spirit upon "all flesh":

> And your sons and your daughters shall prophesy,
>   and your young men shall see visions,
>   and your old men shall dream dreams.
> And moreover upon my servants and upon my handmaids
>   in those days will I pour forth of my Spirit, and
>   they shall prophesy. (Acts 2:17, 18)

Both sons and daughters, servants and handmaids share the
outpouring of the divine gifts. Nor is there any suggestion
that the "handmaids" should be confined to a passive, quiet
role while the male servant prophesied; both men and

women shall prophesy. And women certainly *did* prophesy. In Acts 21:9 "four virgins who had the gift of prophecy," the daughters of Philip the evangelist, are specifically mentioned. But all women were active within the public congregation in the role of prophecy, a function essentially connected with prayer. When St. Paul instructs "every woman who prays or prophesies," to cover her head, he implies that "prophesying by a woman is here on the same plane as prophesying by a man."[1]

There also seem to have been women who taught, at least in an informal way. Priscilla and Aquila took the eloquent but badly instructed Apollos home, "and expounded the Way of God to him more precisely" (Acts 18:26). More important is the famous case of Phoebe, whom Paul commends to the Romans as "our sister, who is in the ministry of the church at Cenchrae." He asks that "you may assist her in whatever business she may have need of you. For she too has assisted many, including myself" (Rom. 16:1). Phoebe's "ministry," it should be said, has been the occasion of much scholarly dispute. The minimalists insist it was but a temporary grace conferred upon Phoebe with no significance for women in general. The maximizers maintain that the Greek words used indicate Phoebe held a position comparable to the presidency of her congregation, and that her vocation and importance should be more of a norm for the apostolic activity of Christian women. The same sort of disputes surround the status of "widows" and "deaconesses" in the early Church. The crucial point is the nature of the work done by all the women whom Paul commends for "working in the Lord." Was the "work" always confined to submissive, silent, menial matters? Most certainly not. Father Jean Daniélou maintains that the Greek words used are the same as those used for men: " 'to work in the Lord' can only refer to apostolic tasks."[2] Women were active in spreading the gospel in a direct and active way.

Indeed, always and everywhere women were eager and enthusiastic converts to Christianity. There are anonymous "women of rank" (Acts 17:4) listed among the early converts, and it is significant that the first European convert to Christianity was the business woman Lydia, a "seller of purple" in Philippi. After she and her household were baptized, "she insisted" that Paul and his companions stay at her house (Acts 16:15). Since he returned to her house from jail in order to encourage the brethren before leaving the city, it would appear that Lydia's house had become the center for the Christians of Philippi. It seems more than likely that Lydia, and other such women, would not be confined to a silent, submissive role in the affairs of the new churches.

Could not one of the reasons for the appeal of Christianity to women be the revolutionary equality given them? When the "perfect law of liberty, the royal law . . . Thou shalt love thy neighbor as thyself" was truly practised, then the world's "partiality towards persons" (James 2:1,8) would disappear. The poor, the enslaved, the uneducated—and women—could, and did enjoy a new freedom within the Christian community. Outside, in the world, Christians were to be circumspect and avoid scandal by adapting themselves when possible to the customs of the time. But within the early Church the "liberty of the sons of God" seems to have been a concrete reality. Women held an important place in the new order, and if inevitably the custom, culture, and the old habits of the world crept in, the radical revolutionary seed of equality had been sown once and briefly flowered in an active, apostolic role for women.

If the practical activity of women in the early Church brought to reality their dignity as persons, so much more did certain other Christian doctrines in an indirect way. Perhaps nothing benefited women so much as the new dignity Christianity gave the human body. Instead of a degrading temporary prison of the soul, the human body by the resurrection of Christ became an eternal temple of the Holy Spirit. Christ had "bought its immortality at a great price"; one's body was destined for eternal life and should now be presented as a "living sacrifice." Chastity, therefore, is no longer urged only for social reasons, but because "the body is for the Lord"; and men as well as women must be chaste—no more double standards in morality.

This idea of the body's dignity helped women in two paradoxical ways. On the one hand, her obvious involvement in basic physical processes, childbirth, nursing, etc., were no longer seen as degrading. Women are no longer "unclean" and in need of purification after childbirth (although superstitions might linger on in this respect). Sexual function was given a new dignity; but, on the other hand, since the body was now to be a temple of the Holy Spirit, it possessed a dignity apart from its sexual function. A woman has importance as a person apart from her sexual role; her body has a value "for the Lord" in itself. She is not incomplete and "wasted" without husband and children. No longer could a woman's body be reduced to a pleasure object or be valued only as a source of offspring. Moreover, virginity for the sake of the kingdom was esteemed—indeed recommended to those who had such a gift. The subsequent growth of the Christian orders of virgins dedicated to God guaranteed woman's dignity by emphasizing her primary and direct relationship to God. In the Christian teaching of the resurrection of the body, woman's dignity as a person was confirmed.

The other great revolutionary tenet of Christianity so beneficial to women was the restoration of marriage. Here too women were elevated to a new dignity. Woman was given an equal right in contracting marriage. The marriage union of husband and wife is created by a *mutual* gift of themselves to each other. As St. Paul says, "the wife has not authority over her body, but the husband; the husband likewise has not authority over his body, but the wife" (I Cor. 7:4). Empowered by God, the husband and wife create an indissoluble union by the gift of themselves to each other. The two become one flesh according to God's original plan. When questioned about divorce, Jesus replies, quoting Genesis:

'For this cause a man shall leave his father and mother, and cleave to his wife, and the two shall become one flesh.' Therefore now they are no longer two, but one flesh. What therefore God has joined together, let no man put asunder. (Mark 10:7-10)

No longer valid is Moses' permission allowing a man to put away his wife. If either husband or wife puts away his spouse and marries another, he or she commits adultery. The two have become one flesh until death, and no whim or motive of expediency can break the bond. The disciples—men of their times—voiced their consternation at this hard teaching by saying, "If the case of a man with his wife is so, it is not expedient to marry" (Matt. 19:10). Significantly, they voiced their incredulity that "the case of a man with his wife" should be so, and not the other way round. It was a revolutionary idea that marriage should be indissoluble; but it was even more disturbing that the man could no longer claim a superior, favored position. When a wife could no longer be divorced arbitrarily, she could assume her rights as an equal partner in marriage. By imposing equal rules for husband and wife, an equality of the two was confirmed.

Such reciprocal and mutual obligations are enumerated in

the various New Testament texts instructing husbands and wives. Those arguing that Christianity espoused the subjugation of women ignore the mutual character of the instructions, but they are there. Distortions are caused by not reading the anti-feminine texts in a full context, and ignoring the fact that humility and obedience were urged for all Christians. For instance, St. Paul says, in Ephesians 5:22: "Let wives be subject to their husbands as to the Lord," but it follows Ephesians 5:21 which says to husband and wife "Be subject to one another in the fear of Christ." When St. Peter enjoins wives "to be subject to their husbands" (I Peter 3:1), it is after instructing all the faithful to "be subject to every human creature for God's sake" (I Peter 2:13). It is good for Christians to obey one another lovingly whenever possible. Similarly, after Peter recommends that women adorn themselves with an "inner life of the heart, in the imperishableness of a quiet and gentle spirit," he extends this unimpeachable Christian ideal to all. Again, in the same instructions, St. Peter speaks of the wife as the "co-heir of the grace of life" (I Peter 3:7), a phrase which both implies equality with the husband and the central importance of Christian grace. "Co-heir" definitely indicates that man and woman are equal, at least in their mutual dependence upon God.

This kind of equality and mutuality is emphasized by St. Paul in an often overlooked passage in I Corinthians. After an argument that seems to be declaring the superiority of man—"For man is not from woman, but woman from man. For man was not created for woman, but woman for man" (11:8, 9)—he adds an all-important qualification:

Yet neither is man independent of woman, nor woman independent of man in the Lord. For as the woman is from the man, so also is the man through the woman, but all things are from God. (I Cor. 11:11, 12)

There could be no better statement of the mutual, reciprocal relationship between man and woman, which in the end is subordinated to their primary relationship to God. Neither man nor woman can claim a clear superiority or independence of the other. They are both equal in their dependence upon God. The important thing is to live the Christian life.

Indeed, the exhortations and teachings of the gospel apply to both men and women. Nothing can be outside the Christian life. "Whether you eat or drink, whatever you do, do for the glory of God." Even such a specialized activity as childbearing must be within the context of general Christian virtues. Timothy says "women will be saved by childbearing, if they continue in faith and love and holiness with modesty" (I, 2:15). The "if" clause transforms a crude biological approach to woman's role, by emphasizing that the important thing for salvation is continuing in faith, love and holiness—virtues necessary for married women, virgins, widows, and men.

If faith and charity are absolutely essential to each Christian, they are even more imperative in the "one flesh" union of marriage. St. Paul exhorts the married pair to mutual charity. The love between husband and wife must be like the love between Christ and His Church. As Christ and the Church are united, so are the husband and the wife. They are "to nourish and cherish" each other as one naturally nourishes and cherishes oneself. Husbands (probably needing it more) are given repeated and explicit exhortations to love their wives: "husbands, love your wives" (Eph. 5:25); "he who loves his own wife loves himself" (Eph. 5:29); "let each one of you also love his wife just as he loves himself"

(Eph. 5:33). Love and the unity of the two-in-one dominate all the instructions to the married.

The unity of husband and wife, the "becoming one flesh," is described as a union paralleling the union of Christ and the Church; man is the head of woman as Christ is the head of the Church. Paul teaches that Christ is the head of His body the Church, and this teaching, the doctrine of the "Mystical Body," is important in Christianity. But it is an involved and complicated doctrine, subject to misunderstandings. The complexity of the doctrine makes it all the more difficult to determine what is meant by the parallel relationship in marriage. How closely does the analogy—man is the head of woman as Christ is the Head of His Church—correspond to the doctrine of the Mystical Body? The text in Ephesians says: "a husband is head of the wife, just as Christ is head of the Church, being himself savior of the body" (Eph. 5:23). The crucial question turns on the meaning of "just as." A literal analogy cannot work since Christ is divine, husbands are not—and Christ, not the husband, saves the wife. How then does the analogy apply?

Is the husband the "head of the wife" only as he is "savior of the body," that is, as the husband is the protector who will "deliver himself up" for his wife? There is work to be done by the theologians defining the meaning or meanings of "the husband as head of the wife." The problem will be more complicated by the text in Corinthians in which St. Paul says that every man is the head of every woman: "But I would have you know that the head of every man is Christ, and the head of the woman is the man, and the head of Christ is God" (I Cor. 11:3). Seemingly, this applies to every man and woman, married or not. Is "head" used in the same way as in the analogy of the Mystical Body and marriage? But the most crucial question of all (and most overlooked) is, how does the phrase "the head of Christ is God" relate to the phrase "the head of the woman is man"? Is Christ to God, as woman to man? Does the relationship of the sexes in some way reflect the unity of the Trinity?

The complications of the question never clouded the crystal-clear interpretations of one strong anti-feminine tradition. Its solution was a simple one—woman was to man as poor sinful humanity (the Church, the body) was to divinity (Christ, the Head). If humanity owed worship to divinity, so did woman owe a kind of worship to man. The "divine right of men" flourished. Such a tidy authoritarian interpretation of the meaning of "head" was inspired not so much by Christianity as by the idea of the secular head of an army, or an Oriental despotic head of state. Initiative, direction and authority went only one way, and woman was at the end of the chain of command. She might have authority over children, servants and animals, but to man she owed unquestioning obedience and passive submission. If all Christians were exhorted to be subject to all, some were to be more subject than others. True freedom for woman could only be found in subjection to man, her master, her divinely ordained head. With these predispositions it was easy to overlook the scriptural passages implying equality of the sexes and their mutual dependence upon each other and God: it was much easier to concentrate on the few negative texts and generalize from them.

The negative texts which justify an inequality of man and woman center around two themes, both drawn, significantly, from the Old Testament. St. Paul sets forth the first theme in his instructions to the Corinthians. He forbids women to speak in church and says "let them be submissive as the Law also says." If they want to learn anything "let them ask their husbands at home, for it is unseemly for a woman to speak in church" (I Cor. 14:35). The main point here is the appeal to the authority of the Judaic Law. It is cited as the authority for woman's submission, but authority or not, its influence upon former Jews would certainly determine what was "unseemly" in women. It may seem surprising to see the great exponent of Christian liberty from the Law citing the Law to suppress women. But in this connection it is well to remember that St. Peter needed a vision from heaven to persuade him to free new Christians from the Judaic dietary laws. The best of men can be inconsistent when discarding old ways to provide new wineskins for new wine.

The second anti-feminine theme derived from the Old Testament is more serious. In Timothy, the reason why women are not to teach or exercise authority over men is explained thus: "Adam was formed first, then Eve. And Adam was not deceived, but the woman was deceived and was in sin" (I Tim. 2:13, 14). Man is superior because he was created first; "woman was created for man," and woman must be submissive because she shares the greater guilt of Eve. Last formed, first fallen, woman deserves her subjection to man. She is the "weaker vessel," and in this reference St. Peter most probably meant "weaker" in more than the physical sense, for he holds up Sara's obedience to Abraham as a pattern for Christian wives. Shades of the Law's influence again! In the end, the Law and a special interpretation of Genesis influenced the anti-feminine texts in the New Testament. Woman's subordination in the New Testament is justified by appeals to the Old Testament. This relationship of the old to the new has often been recognized; it has even been characterized as the Christian transmission of the "savagely anti-feminine" Judaic tradition. But was it really a "savagely anti-feminine"[3] tradition? A glance at women in the Old Testament is in order at this point.

A cursory look through the Old Testament would seem to prove that women were thought of and treated as inferiors. Inequality was the practice from the very beginning of life; a woman bearing a son was "unclean" for 33 days, but after giving birth to a daughter she was "unclean" for 66 days. Quantitatively this would make boys twice as valuable as girls. And males were given twice the autonomy and privilege. Every young girl was subject to the authority of her father, until given by him to a husband who then became her master. Since a husband in early times could take more than one wife, a woman's position as wife was an insecure one. She could always be "put away" with little ado. The double standard of conduct was thoroughly institutionalized. The extent of masculine privilege is shown by the ordeal for a suspected adultress detailed in Numbers 5: even when lacking proof of a wife's infidelity—or even "if a man is overcome by a feeling of jealousy that makes him suspect his wife, whether she was actually impure or not" (Num. 5:13)—a husband can apply "the law of jealousy." The woman makes a cereal offering, stands before the priest and finally takes a potent, bitter drink—a drink which will not harm the pure, but which will so curse an adultress that her "belly will swell and her thighs will waste away" (Num. 5:27). Needless to say, there is no provision for unfaithful husbands or any concern for a wife's feelings of jealousy. While a husband lived, he ruled. Only as a widow did a woman obtain some autonomy. In contrast with a maid or wife, a widow could make a vow to the Lord or pledge her word without being overruled by a man.

It was not just that women were treated as if they were minors; they were also the object of much scorn. The books of traditional Judaic wisdom are peppered with anti-feminine diatribes. The message is simple: women are dangerous. Being weak, unfaithful and seductive, they easily lead men astray. Wise men will not be seduced by the beauty of women; it is better not even to look at them, and certainly one should not tarry among them. Woman's malice is above all other malice, her anger worse, her wickedness totally destructive. She contaminates even the good, and in the judgment of one sage, "better is the iniquity of a man, than a woman doing a good turn . . ." (Ecclus. 42:14). The source of all this potentiality for evil is woman's identification with Eve. It is as the daughter of that first woman that she is indicted. The damning truth is that "from the woman came the beginning of sin, and by her we all die" (Ecclus. 25:33).

If these passages and the patriarchal legislation regarding women represented a complete picture, then Judaic antifeminism could well be characterized as "savage." But the truth is that, in the Old Testament as in the New, there is an inconsistent attitude, for there exists a positive as well as a negative understanding of woman. In the Old Testament, woman is often recognized as an equal creation of God. A woman could be a handmaid of the Lord and offer to Him her worship and vows. She took part in the worship of the people and was expected to observe the moral commandments of God. While she stood on an unequal footing before the Law, she was nevertheless granted certain rights and protected to some degree. She could never be taken to be solely a possession.

Even the unequal marriage arrangements were often mitigated by love. The wives of many patriarchs were beloved and wielded a great deal of influence—and this despite the polygamy which seems to have been a burden for everyone concerned. The quarreling and the jealousy among wives and their children brought only dissension; and, in this respect, competition in bearing sons caused special bitterness.

Still, the rivalry for sons often appears to have been a purely feminine affair: a lack of children did not influence the love of a devoted husband. Elcana, the husband of heartbroken, childless Anna, wistfully tried to console her in the face of taunts from his less-loved but fertile other wife: "And why dost thou afflict thy heart? Am I not better to thee than ten children?" (1 Samuel 8). But Anna was not comforted, and beseeched the Lord for a child. Her prayers were answered and she bore Samuel and dedicated him to God. Anna is one type of the good woman in the Old Testament. Her faith and prayers are rewarded in the conception of a son. She exults in the power of the Lord to do all things: He has made the barren fruitful.

Good women appear not only in the narratives of the Old Testament, but praise of them is also ensconced in the Wisdom literature. Often the praise of good women will directly follow an anti-feminine diatribe. But whether in praise or blame, the opinion is made all the more forceful by the delightful Semitic imagery. The "grace of a diligent woman" shall not only "delight her husband," but it will also "fat his bones" (Ecclus. 26:17). A good woman's beauty is the "ornament of her house," and she is compared to a "shining lamp," "a pillar of rest" or the rising sun. But the good woman is not good simply because she fats her husband's bones; she derives her goodness primarily from her relationship with God. "Her discipline is the gift of God" (Ecclus. 26:17). In fact, "as everlasting foundations upon a solid rock, so are the commandments of God in the heart of a holy woman" (Ecclus. 26:21). The good woman's holiness is founded, as is man's, upon her obedience to God. The vertical relationship with God precedes the horizontal one to her husband: if she is "a help like to himself," she, like man, derives her strength from the Lord.

Perhaps the most famous portrait of a good woman in the Old Testament comes in the oft-quoted verses in Proverbs describing the "valiant woman." Everyone touches on this passage when discussing Christian and Judaic attitudes toward women, but often in a way which does not clarify its meaning. Often the indignant feminist and the Christian apologist come up with the same interpretation—these verses describe the "good housewife." For the feminist, the good housewife may be anathema (woman confined to domesticity); or she may be glorified by the apologist (woman's highest function lies in homemaking). But in their common interpretation they reduce the valiant woman to a caricature. More than a housewife is described in such verses as these:

She hath girded her loins with strength, and hath strengthened her arm.
Strength and beauty are her clothing and she shall laugh in the latter day.
She hath opened her mouth to wisdom, and the law of clemency is on her tongue.
She hath opened her hand to the needy, and stretched out her hands to the poor. (Proverbs 31:10-30)

This woman is strong, wise and merciful; and her strength comes from the Lord. Her dominant characteristics are those of the Godly, whether they be male or female. In her strength and wisdom the valiant woman may be an edifying example of femininity in any age.

Moreover, it is hardly accurate to call her a "housewife" in our sense of the term today. The work she does has little relevance to the situation of the modern woman. There are few women today who have a husband who "sitteth among the senators of the land." Nor can the modern housewife emulate the valiant woman's care for "all her domestics."

There are few servants today, and there is neither time nor money to "consider a field and buy it," or to "plant a vineyard," or to produce fine linen to trade with foreign merchants. What we see in the valiant woman is a prominent upper-class lady running a huge household in which the domestic establishment overlaps commercial enterprises—in the manner of a medieval manor or master craftsman's house. It is thus hardly surprising that such a woman in such a household could play a very active part in the world outside of the home: the valiant woman is one whose "works praise her in the gates." Her whole community can join with her children and husband to "call her blessed."

Despite her limitations as a contemporary model, the very existence of the valiant woman in the Old Testament—along with the praises sung to good women—shows that there existed a positive idea of the feminine in Judaism. The undoubted prejudice against women as the source of sin and death is thus counter-balanced by another image. As in the story of Ruth and Esther, faithful women are again and again shown as the bringers of blessings. Still more, there are two other women who exemplify an even more exalted vision of woman. The heroines Deborah and Judith served God and saved their people by their active leadership in war. Significantly, they served God directly, outside of a domestic framework. In the doing of God's will they not only co-operated with men, but commanded them as well.

Deborah, the earlier heroine, is a unique leader of her people both in war and peace. She is described as "the prophetess Deborah," "wife of Laphidoth," "a mother in Israel." In times of peace she "used to sit under Deborah's palm tree" where "the Israelites came up to her for judgment" (Judges 4:4,5). In obedience to the Lord, Deborah initiates and plans a campaign. She sends for the warrior Barac and

assures him that she will accompany him to war—he won't go
without her. When a great victory is won, it is celebrated by
the famed Canticle of Deborah. In the song, Deborah boasts
that the Lord gave her the power to arouse Israel from cow-
ardice: "the people of the Lord came down for me as warriors." Before Deborah, the warriors had been staying close
to their hearths, passively "listening to the lowing of the
herds" (Judges 5:16), for

> When I, Deborah, rose,
>> when I rose, a mother in Israel,
>
> New gods were their choice;
>> then the war was at their gates.
>
> Not a shield could be seen, not a lance,
>> among forty thousand in Israel!

After Deborah, "Freedom beyond the walls" was restored
and "the land was at rest for forty years." Oppression was
overthrown, peace was restored, but one is left to wonder
whether Deborah returned to her palm and her judgments.

If there is a dearth of detail about Deborah, another feminine triumph in the war which Deborah initiated against
Sisara and his army was celebrated at length. Sisara, defeated
and in flight, comes to the tent of Jahel. Inviting him in, she
gives him milk, tucks him to sleep under a rug, and promises
to stand guard. But all this nurturing motherliness is dis-
pelled once Sisara sleeps, for then

> With her left hand she reached for the peg,
>> with her right, for the workman's mallet.
>
> She hammered Sisara, crushed his head;
>> she smashed, stove in his temple.

At her feet he sank down, fell, lay still. . . .

Blessed among women be Jahel,
blessed among tent-dwelling women.
(Judges 5:24-27)

Since Jahel is known only for wielding her tent peg and
mallet, she does not contribute much toward an ideal femininity. But she does, along with Deborah, raise doubts about
the supposedly inherent tenderness of the eternal woman.

Judith, the other great heroine of her people, is a little
more tender-hearted, but just as effective in cutting off Holofernes' head. She finds it necessary to pray for "constancy in
my mind, that I may despise him: and fortitude that I may
overthrow him." But, the deed done, Judith bundles the
severed head into a sack and coolly walks out of the enemy
camp back to her besieged city. Once there, she holds the
head high and proclaims the power of the Lord. An allied
soldier standing by faints away (when he recuperates he is
converted immediately), but Judith calmly directs the strat-
egy which will accomplish the thorough rout of Holofernes'
army. Her plan works perfectly and Judith reigns as a heroine of her people for the rest of her life. The people call her
"blessed among women," the high priests and the ancients
proclaim "thou hast done manfully," and the sons of Israel
exult that "the Persians quaked at her constancy, and the
Medes at her boldness."

It has been objected that Judith was only a one-time
assassin[4]—and so no real example of a woman taking an active, respected and important role in the world. But this view
takes at face value Judith's beautiful protestations of humility without appreciating them. The prayers and songs of
Judith are magnificent and are reminiscent of the praises of

God found in Exodus and traditionally associated with Miriam. Judith is a holy woman who, in her humility, attributes all to God. But she has prepared for her great saving deed by a widowhood dedicated to prayer, fasting and good deeds. At the crucial moment, she possesses not only beauty and wealth, but also wisdom and holiness. Her authority is such that she rebukes the leaders of her besieged city, advises them, and then carries out her own plan. With a courageous confidence in the Lord she triumphs over every evil; and it seems obvious that she wields much influence for the rest of her life.

Judith, like Deborah, is a handmaid of the Lord. Their service to Him is direct and bypasses the authority of men. It is also independent of childbearing and childrearing. Nor is there any passive, hidden quality to their work for the Lord. When called by God, the handmaid is submissive to God and thereby assumes equality with, and even authority over, men. She obeys God, commands men and achieves the salvation of her people.

Saviors of the people, or weak and guilty daughters of Eve, rightfully suppressed—how are these contradictory appraisals to be reconciled? In the Old Testament, the institutionalized suppression of women counters the assertion of woman's equal value as a person, so that while the Judaic tradition is not "savagely" anti-feminine, it is anti-feminine, with important exceptions. In the New Testament, on the other hand, what is but a promise in the Old Testament finally flowers in the Christian good news: "In Christ there is neither male nor female." The Christian unity of love leaves no room for discrimination or inequality. The inconsistent and minor prejudice against women remaining in the New Testament is a culturally conditioned derivation from the dominant anti-feminism of Judaism. But it can give rise to a crucial question: does the Christian bias against women, inherited from the culture and the Law, have any meaning? This brings us back again to Eve. The negative assessment of Eve's role in the creation and fall of man is the theological basis of all scriptural anti-feminism, whether in the Old Testament or in the New. Eve, or "the woman" of the Genesis story, is crucial in any Christian doctrine of femininity. Only when Christ was born of "a woman" did another more important one appear.

NOTES

[1] Jean Daniélou, S.J., *The Ministry of Women in the Early Church* (London: The Faith Press, Ltd., 1961), p. 9.

[2] *Ibid.*, p. 8.

[3] Simone de Beauvoir, *The Second Sex* (New York: Bantam Books, 1961), p. 90.

[4] *Ibid.*, p. 121.

THREE

"From the Old Eve to the New Woman"

Eve is inescapable in any search for a Christian view of woman. Every negative text in both the Old and the New Testament, and the anti-feminine tradition springing from them, justifies discrimination against women by pointing to *Genesis* and Eve. The prosecution charges that God created woman subordinate to man and then confirmed woman's lower place as punishment for Eve's greater guilt in the Fall. Genesis provides both proof and charter for establishing a hierarchy of the sexes: God Himself approves the primacy of the male.

Consider the order of creation. The thrust of the argument is that man's primary creation in time implied a primary status. Man was created by God for Himself: woman was created to fulfill man's needs. She is a concession to his loneliness, a divine afterthought. While "man is in some sort the direct reflection of the divine majesty," woman "is like the image of an image."[1] This subordination and secondhand fashioning arises from her creation from Adam's rib. Much is made of that rib. Bossuet, among many others, was sure that Eve had been created from a "superfluous" rib. The moral was clear: man was created in God's image and placed in the world to do God's work (naming the animals, dressing the garden). Woman, on the other hand, had no independent purpose or work other than helping man. Man has a direct relationship to God, but woman in her life and work is to be dependent upon man. Even the great Carmelite philosopher, Edith Stein, followed the tradition: "It is man's nature to serve his cause directly, whereas woman serves it for his sake, and so it is fit that she should do so under his guidance."[2] The very order of nature, even before the Fall, is said to ordain the primacy of the masculine sex. In Paradise (according to Milton) Eve joyfully acclaimed Adam, "my Guide and Head," without whom I "am to no end . . . God is thy Law, thou mine."[3]

The subtle serpent, following in this old tradition, realizes the frailty of woman: he tempts Eve when she is alone. Adam, supposedly, would have had the strength to resist his lies. It was the woman's seductive persuasion which led man into sin, in a typical feminine maneuver. "Do you not know," Tertullian wrote, "that each of you is also an Eve? . . . you are the devil's gateway, you are the unsealer of that forbidden tree, you are the first deserter of the divine law, you are the one who persuaded him whom the devil was too weak to attack. How easily you destroyed man, the image of God! Because of the death which you brought upon us, even the Son of God had to die. . . ."[4]

Today such charges are muted. But one has their modern counterpart in psychological analyses of woman's greater emotionality, inherited from Eve. "Every woman has a touch about her of this Eve," wrote Jean Mouroux in 1948. "This unsubmissiveness, that is to say a certain egoistic independence—half-concealed, caressing, but none the less obstinate, stubborn and dangerous—is the subtle temptation of the weaker and less heavily carnal vessel. . . . For the woman is loved and knows it, and is tempted to presume on this love to get herself pampered, served and adored even to the point of betrayal of God."[5] In Eve's case, her womanly "logic of desire," an "integral part of her passivity," refused to submit to man's "logic of reason."[6] And so it goes. Eve is still the symbol "of all the failings of humanity";[7] as Eve persuaded Adam, so all women can tempt all men.

There is more. In the aftermath of the Fall, God confirmed and intensified woman's subordination to man both as punishment for her greater guilt and to guard the right order of the world. "Distress in childbearing" and the "dominion of the husband" shall for all time be the just punishment meted out to women. The dominion of the rational male will also safeguard mankind from a disastrous indulgence in feminine emotionalism and instability. Never again should God have to reproach husbands as He did Adam after the Fall: "Because you have listened to your wife . . ." (Gen. 3:17). The conclusion from all of this is inevitable. Last formed, first fallen, always more vulnerable, woman must accept her subordinate and complementary role in creation. There is a "divinely ordained hierarchy in the relationship between man and woman . . . which it is essential to preserve and reinstate."[8]

But is it really so simple? Must one deduce a "divinely ordained hierarchy" from the Genesis story? There are good reasons to think otherwise, especially if Genesis is examined afresh without prior assumptions of masculine primacy. First of all, take the claim that woman was created from the beginning for a subordinate role, an assertion which takes for granted that it is better to be created first (out of dust) than second (out of bone). Such assumptions are never made by thinkers impressed by the fact and idea of evolution. Even without a knowledge of evolution, it is just as logical to maintain that it is better to be formed later, as man was formed after and not before the animals. As an Elizabethan "Apologie for Women" puts it, "Every worke being still more perfect then other, still ending in the most perfect of all, He rested as having finished all in her, beyond whose perfection no creature more could be added, created, or imagined."[9] Assumptions brought to the story can decide the case either way, but there does not seem to be any internal evidence in the creation story itself to posit man's primacy on his prior creation. Besides, in the first mention of mankind's creation in Genesis I, it is simply stated that "male and female he created them." Eve's creation in Genesis 2 can hardly be labelled a divine afterthought. Nor can Eve be called a concession to man's loneliness; for even within Genesis 2 God decides to create a helper "like himself," *before* Adam discovers his uniqueness among the animals. Woman, too, is a direct reflection of God's will with a direct, independent relationship to God.

The creation of woman from Adam's rib, therefore, does not necessarily prove her subordinate state. What then does the rib signify? There are some complicated psychoanalytical theories that see the account of Adam's rib-birth of Eve as a reversed Oedipal fantasy, reminiscent of primitive puberty rites in which males simulate childbirth.[10] Such strained and involved psychoanalytical interpretations can only be equalled by the involved medieval speculations upon the subordinate or superfluous status of the rib used. Both approaches are unsatisfactory, for the real point seems to be the one made by Cardinal Léger in discussing the creation story. He reports that scholars have shown that "the Sumerian word 'TI' and its corresponding hieroglyph can mean equally 'rib' and 'life' "; and he concludes that "the episode of Genesis II would therefore mean that woman was made out of the very 'life' of man . . . the identity of nature between man and woman is being stressed."[11] Adam confirms this identity by his words: "She now is bone of my bone, and flesh of my flesh"; and the sacred writer adds the comment "and the two become one flesh" (Gen. 2:24). Furthermore, identity is again stressed, according to Cardinal Léger, because given the Semitic importance of names, "the fact that woman received a name so closely resembling that of man (ish, isha) signifies, once again, equality of man and woman in dignity and nature."[12]

The important thing about woman in the Genesis story is that she is an equal part of an organic unit, a "helper *like* himself" without a differentiated role. "Helper" indicates no inferiority, according to one scholar, for in the 21 times it is found in the Old Testament, helper (ezer) in 16 cases "indicates a superior who assists us."[13] As an equal helper, there is no limitation of her help to man who will do God's work; woman like man can "till the garden" and "name the animals." She, as a member of "mankind," is to have dominion over the animals and to "be fruitful and multiply; fill the earth and subdue it" (Gen. 1:28). Here it is important to note that male and female are *both* "to multiply" and *both* "to subdue the earth." Women are not to be fruitful and multiply in seclusion while men do the work of the world. Both sexes of mankind are given the privileges and responsibilities of the dominion of the earth. Neither the subordination of woman nor differentiation of sexual roles seemed to exist in Paradise.

But what of the time after the beginning? Was the Fall of man more the fault of the woman than the man? And did she receive a greater punishment as "the gateway of death"? Here again only prior anti-feminine assumptions prove the greater guilt of Eve. The biblical account says simply that, deceived by the Serpent, Eve "took of its fruit and ate it, and also gave some to her husband and he ate" (Gen. 3:6). But what embellishments have been created for this line's interpretation! One can choose between assumptions that Adam was totally innocent and ignorant of what he did, or elsewhere read of Eve persuading, seducing and arguing in order to entice him. There is even an ultra-romantic interpretation in which Adam, realizing Eve is lost, gallantly damns himself for her sake. (Milton's Adam declares "for with thee certain my resolution is to Die."[14]) None of this seems justified by the actual account. Again it is the unity of the man and woman that is stressed. Only after both have eaten, were "the eyes of both" opened, and "they hid themselves."

It is the cunning serpent rather than Eve who emerges as the seducer of the story. Whatever the significance of the serpent, whether symbol of idolatrous fertility cult or personification of Lucifer, it is he rather than Eve who does the seducing. St. Ambrose was even of a mind that in the Fall "there is more excuse for the woman" who was tempted "by an angel . . . superior to a human being," and, he notes, in repentance the woman's excuse "was inspired by a more general feeling, since she blames the serpent; whereas Adam defends himself to God by accusing his companion."[15] But with all thanks to St. Ambrose, efforts to assign the greater blame for the Fall miss the story's emphasis upon the couple as a unit who are equally guilty.

Equal guilt merits equal punishment, and contrary to tradition Eve's punishment does not seem so much greater than Adam's. After all, Adam's curse includes "cursed ground," "thorns," "thistles," and "death." Is this so much better than pain in childbirth, and the husband's dominion? In fact, since pain, death, disordered nature, and the domination of the strong over the weak are general ills of mankind, the curses of Genesis can plausibly be read as a descriptive account of the general frustration of creation produced by the entry of evil into the world. However, if the curses are pro-scriptive rather than primarily descriptive, this does estab-lish the fact that the husband's dominion is at best an evil, like pain and death, reluctantly introduced into God's plan for mankind.

Modern theologians, reassessing the exegesis of Genesis, now declare that before the Fall the husband did not have dominion. Those who would see woman originally created as subordinate are, "missing the importance of the contrast which the story points between woman as God made her and woman as she existed. In Hebrew society also woman was a depressed class: the storyteller was not attempting a femininist reform, but he wished to state that in the beginning it was not so."[16] Karl Rahner declares that the sacred writer in Genesis is revealing the equality of woman, and he has little sympathy with those who see the formation of Eve from Adam's rib as sign of her subordination.[17] The whole trend of recent theology reveals that anti-feminine prejudice, aris-ing in a masculine dominated world, has retroactively read patriarchy into Paradise. It is also likely that the actual, de-graded state of marriage influenced the interpretations of the scriptural curse of husband's dominion. The curse of pain in childbirth was similarly misinterpreted for centuries. Pope Pius XII pointed out these misinterpretations in a speech approving modern methods of painless childbirth.

Interpretations of Scripture are always affected by the state of society and the amount of knowledge available at the time. This was especially true before the development of an his-torical consciousness in biblical studies. This consciousness in current biblical studies has not only changed the interpre-tation of the creation story, but has also helped to reveal the cultural setting of the anti-feminine texts in the New Testament. Knowledge of the particular culture and the problems of the young Church helps to explain some of the rules made against women, but more important, current theology provides a principle for judging New Testament references to the Old Testament. A citation by a New Testament writer of a passage from the Old Testament, Karl Rahner has written, is "a literary genre of its own." It is thus necessary to "assess a citation by its source"; Christ's reference to Jonah in the whale, for instance, by no means guarantees the literal, historical truth of the book of Jonah.

This principle is particularly important in judging New Testament references to women; for the pessimistic, repressive texts refer back to Genesis and embody an anti-feminine interpretation of the creation story. As Father Rahner asks: "Is it really possible to use I Cor. 11:8-12; Eph. 5:28-30; I Tim. 2:13 to prove the 'literal' interpretation of the story in Genesis of the formation of Eve from Adam's rib?"[17] Once the old interpretation of woman's subordinate creation is questioned, then the negative New Testament texts must give way to the revolutionary New Testament texts. Recent biblical scholarship has recovered the emphasis of the sacred writer of Genesis upon woman's equality, and so confirmed as the dominant Christian teaching St. Paul's assertion: "In Christ there is neither . . . male nor female." If, in the beginning, man and woman were equal before their Creator, surely in Christ woman regains the equality of Eden.

But before new theological and scriptural studies exonerated Eve, the concept of Mary as the New Eve did much to restore woman's dignity. If Eve was blamed for initiating the Fall, Mary could be praised for initiating our salvation by her *Fiat*—"Be it done unto me." A woman's obedience cancelled the first woman's disobedience, and she, virgin-mother of the Savior, becomes the gateway to life. As the New Eve,

Mary is the woman whose seed shall destroy the serpent. Just as Christ, the new Adam, brings life to all mankind instead of death, she it is who restores the dignity of woman. She it is who, through her miraculous childbirth, reverses Eve's distress in childbearing. As a beautiful prayer in the Roman Rite's "Churching of Women" expresses this truth: God, "through the delivery of the blessed Virgin Mary, has turned into joy the pains of the faithful in childbirth."

This is as far as the parallel of Eve and Mary is usually carried. Mary's virginal maternity and marriage are not seen as a reversal of the remaining punishment of Eve: "For your husband shall be your longing, though he have dominion over you." Mary's "lack of longing" is asserted in the doctrine of her perpetual virginity, but the dominion of Joseph her husband is, for some reason, rarely questioned. Christian women can be called to imitate Mary's virginity, but Mary with all Christian wives will, with Eve, submit to masculine authority.

Unfortunately, other old ideas are also included in the concept of Mary as the New Eve. Once the "New Eve" argument begins with the old assumption of Eve's subordination and greater guilt in the Genesis story, two other distortions quickly follow. The first is the separation of Mary from the Church and history. As Eve was separated from Adam and made solely responsible for sin, so Mary became separated from Christ. The insistence that Mary was the actual "Mother of God" began as a movement to safeguard Christ's divinity, but it later grew into an autonomous cult. Indeed, a theologian like Father Josef Jungmann tells us, an exaggerated Mariology reflected but the long fight against Arianism that made the whole Church overemphasize Christ's divinity and undervalue his humanity. Even today, Karl Rahner and Yves Congar claim, the reigning crypto-heresy is monophysitism—the people do not fully realize Christ's humanity and his role as Mediator. When Christ's humanity is forgotten, attention is transferred to Mary; she then becomes the human link to her divine, but remote and unapproachable, Son. She, rather than Christ, is human mediatrix to awesome Divinity.

It is ironic, however, that Mary's humanity also then recedes from view. In the exaggerated forms of the Marian cult, Mary becomes a combination of the great Mother Goddess and Pallas Athena, far removed from the actual woman who lived in Nazareth. Consequently, the adulation and glorification of Mary do not necessarily help actual woman's position in society. Cathedrals and gorgeous art work dedicated to Mary as Queen did not keep women from being thoroughly suppressed. In fact, one could make a good case that the more prominent the Marian cult in a culture, the more feeble will be women's civil rights and effective freedom. Perhaps this is an unfair generalization from the Latin countries today, but it does seem that exaggerated Marian devotions serve as a cultural compensation for masculine-run societies with rigid double standards. The New Eve may be exalted, and even Woman in the abstract glorified, but all other women living here and now, must be kept away from business, education, the professions, government, and (heaven forbid) the altar. Imprisonment upon a pedestal is as effective as any other.

A further exaggeration in the "New Eve" approach to Mary is found in some common assertions about Mary's femininity and her feminine role as a model for all women. Mary is often portrayed as a sweet, passive, undemanding mother and humble housewife. She is all tenderness and mercy with a purity untouched by the world. In popular piety she is sometimes said to pull into heaven by the rosary sinners who would otherwise be damned. She weeps, too, when young Catholic ladies whistle. This kind of sentimentality so surrounds the image of Mary, that any possibility of clearly perceiving her theological maternity is engulfed by what Marc Oraison cites as so dangerous a religious state for the child, "a childish dependence upon an emotional, sensibly protective maternity."[18] Mary is often made the embodiment of the undemanding, accepting, nurturing Mother, when she is not pictured as the timid, distant Virgin (neither form of passive femininity demanding much effort or response). Since Mary is this way, the argument seems to go, surely all women should also remain sweet, passive, hidden and contemplative. If Mary was "the heart" of the home at Nazareth, and is now "the heart" of the Church, then women are to be "the heart" of the home and the world. If Mary only "pondered these things in her heart," then her daughters are to do no more. Mary is at the "head of the inconspicuous, hidden saintly women"[19] whose "world is not the blatant one of public life." Woman as the New Eve "by Fiat is made a helpmate";[20] that is, "she stands in the shadows going forward behind the veil."[21]

But in the context of contemporary biblical theology, a very different and more satisfying view of Mary appears. Mary can no longer be separated from the Church or history. She becomes the pre-eminent member of the Church, privileged because of her great faith. In her physical maternity, Mary is uniquely blessed, but even more, "Blessed is she who believed" (Luke 1:45). All Christians must echo her "Fiat," as they hope to follow her Assumption. She not only heralds the future of the Church, but is the link with the Old Testament. Abraham through faith went out from his people and offered his son to God; Mary is the physical descendant and the spiritual daughter of Abraham's faith. God's promise to

all who have believed is kept with her, but she is the fulfillment of the holy women of the Old Testament as well. Did
not Mary also conceive by the Lord's will in an even more
miraculous and unique way than Anna? And like Deborah
and Judith, Mary leads her people in vanquishing the enemy.
The Liturgy fills the feasts of Mary with passages from the
great stories of Deborah and Judith.

Biblical scholarship too has given new meaning to the
words, "But Mary kept all these things and pondered them
in her heart" (Luke 2:19,51). This verse has been used senti-
mentally as an example of exemplary feminine response;
women following Mary are to ponder in their hearts, i.e., passively accept and contemplate truth rather than initiate activity in the world. Yet in a recent detailed analysis of this
verse, a biblical scholar concludes that its purpose is to "un-
derscore the coming of messianic salvation as a divine work
surpassing human understanding," for it is "modelled on Old
Testament texts Daniel 7,28 and Genesis 37,11."[22] Since in
the Old Testament texts Daniel and Jacob "ponder" God's
truth, to make "pondering" an intuitive, particularly feminine response is pure fabrication. If Daniel, Jacob, and Mary,
the representative of Israel, pondered and kept these things
in their hearts, so should every Christian whether male or
female. It has nothing to do with woman's role.

Indeed, Mary's *fiat* was the beginning of the great battle,
and it is right to describe her as "terrible as an army dressed
in battle array." The daughter of the prophets in her "Mag-
nificat" exults in God's avenging justice: "He has shown
might with his arm"; He has "scattered the proud," "put
down the mighty," and "the rich he has sent empty away"
(Luke 1:51-53). Mary's faith results in a consuming zeal to
follow God's will, and like John the Baptist her humility includes prophetic fire. Submissiveness to God does not imply

retiring timidity; Mary may well have been a spirited and demanding woman, capable of the righteous anger and irony Christ so often displayed.

Scripture says nothing whatever about Mary's "sweetness," nor does it show her as particularly retiring. She courageously pronounces her "Fiat" and then goes "in haste" to help her cousin Elizabeth. When her time comes, she must bear her child among strangers far from home. It requires strength to be alone with mystery and prepare for "the sword which will pierce your heart." When Christ grows to be a man, she not only initiates his miraculous ministry at Cana, but once comes to take Him home. Finally, only the most courageous woman could go out to Golgotha and witness the execution of her Son. How appropriate that Mary should be present to receive the Pentecostal fire. "The lowliness of his handmaid" does not preclude aggressive strength and efficiency (such as that of the Valiant Woman in Proverbs) or a public ministry: "His handmaids shall prophesy." This unique handmaid, identified with wisdom, and "clothed with the sun," cannot at the same time lead other women to a "hidden inconspicuous life" "behind the veil," or "in the shadows." All talk of Mary as the passive and "hidden heart" of the Church, as of the little home in Nazareth, seems inappropriate.

The basic flaw in the speculations presented as descriptions of the Holy Family's idyllic home life is the naive assumption that cultures differ very little. Mary is always pictured as the humble, obedient housewife and hovering mother, whose activities and attitudes reflect the author's own preconceptions of what women in his own culture should be and do. Such effusive apocrypha bring to mind nothing so much as the incongruous Renaissance paintings of the Annunciation in which Mary sits in a Renaissance palace and receives

Gabriel with courtly fifteenth-century courtesy. Some sophistication about different cultures, customs and the actual realities of Semitic life in first-century Palestine might curb such exaggerations. Perhaps the Holy Family was an "extended family," living communally with many relatives, with all those "brothers [i.e., cousins] of the Lord" coming in and out. They may have lived very, very simply in a household in which cleanliness was not next to Godliness. Other family customs were certainly very different. Many a modern parent could envy, if not emulate, a trip in which a twelve-year-old would not be missed for a day's journey. Caravans full of "relatives and friends" differ from the family car as much as a poor craftsman's village home differs from the modern technologically equipped home—and different behavior is appropriate in each.

The point of course is that neither Mary's actual daily activities, nor speculative constructs of her as humble housewife and nurturing mother, can be held up to modern women as models of behavior. After all, no one insists that Christian men become carpenters, but that they imitate Christ's perfect obedience and love of God.

Mary, too, "believed" and obeyed, and her example applies to men and women. Her virtues prove that the essentials of Christian behavior are above sexual distinctions, sexual roles and family relationships. Christ, "looking around on those who were sitting about him," said most pointedly, "For whoever does the will of God, he is my brother and sister and mother" (Mark 3:35). Mothers and sisters do not imitate Mary while brothers and fathers follow Christ. Women do not "choose to be either Eve or Mary." This common, pious platitude, upon which the whole parallelism of Eve and Mary rests, implies that Christ saves men while Mary saves women. (This is almost as bad as the theory that Christ saves Mary who saves everybody else.) No; women must choose Christ and live in Christ just as men do. Women cannot be identified as Old Eves or New Eves; they are neither better nor worse than men. As far as the Christian life and salvation is concerned, men and women are simply human beings.

Why then has so much recent Catholic writing about women consistently insisted that women have a different vocation from men just because they are women? Poets, popes, psychologists, popular writers, and theologians stress over and over that every woman must partake of the eternal feminine. The "essence of woman" may be a bit vaguely defined, but it is always described as the opposite of rational, aggressive, abstract, thrusting masculinity. Men are assumed to be stable and independent, but woman "is ambiguous . . . she is saint or sinner, angel or devil."[23] Every woman oscillates in her relations with men between these two attitudes, i.e., "mate and temptress."[24] As either saint or sinner "woman craves support, control, a master,"[25] because her nature is receptive, passive, emotional, sensitive, concrete and nurturing. She is "essentially nature," "while man is essentially act."[26] Woman knows instinctively that being is so much more important than doing, for within her body she possesses delicate and subtle psychohormonic harmony and lunar rhythms; "she is much more a part of the cosmos and its respiration than we are."[27] When woman is true to her true self, she imitates Mary the New Eve in leading man to heaven. "The eternal feminine" is the spiritual sex made for love and contemplation (behind the veil that is). All women should try to be the hidden heart of the home, the silent heart of the Church, the acquiescent heart of the world. Her highest fulfillment is to complement man and provide "the place where man returns to find comfort, inspiration and a sense of the timeless."[28] Every woman is to be to man "at once ideal, helpmate and mother."[29]

But why be repetitive? Reams of such quotations about women are all too available. What is behind this insistence that woman is so different? A faulty exegesis of scriptural references to women is certainly one source, but it hardly accounts for such an elaborate, full-blown tradition. No, the traditional theology of woman is part and parcel of a theology of sex. Interpretation of femininity and feminine roles will be based on assumptions about the meaning of sexual differences and sexual life. Why did God "create them male and female"; what is the meaning of human sexuality? How important is sex and sexual identity?

Not very, some will reply. All the important people in the Church from our Lord down have given it up; celibacy is the better way to salvation. God only created sex and the sexes for procreation, and Christ has told us there will be no marriage in heaven. All will be "as the angels" in heaven because, unfortunately, no matter how hard married people try, "sexual experiences have, of themselves, something of a stupefying nature, in the strong sense of the term."[30] In the great majority of cases sexual life inevitably "results in a too great preoccupation with the things of sense."[31] Christ may have redeemed marriage somewhat, but alas, "the union of the sexes is still the focal point of sin," since it can "only give birth to beings who will one day meet death."[32] (And these are modern-day quotations!)

In this pessimistic view of sex, the main emphasis is negative: sexuality is *the* main distraction from the spiritual life and man's chief temptation. Since male celibates are those who usually express this pessimism, it is not surprising that it includes a deep suspicion of women. Woman in the ideal may be exalted to a distant summit, but concrete women—who are all too obviously involved in sexual functions—must be classified as "very different" and urged to accept a segregated, subordinate position. A naive assumption of masculine superiority and right of dominion carries the day. After all, God became incarnate as a *man* and appointed *men* as His apostles. Men were meant by God to be the authoritative, aggressive initiators, leaders of the Church and the world. Women are to be the passive followers. Women must realize that "femininity is a sign of the essential incompleteness of the creature."[33] Since body and soul are one and women's bodies are so (dangerously) different, there are masculine souls and feminine souls, each with very different vocations.

When presented with this view, one has the impression that its proponents have never freed themselves from primitive sexual taboos, or more important, have never been able for one minute to survey objectively their own cultural formation. They are still worried that ancient paganism exalted sex and old heresies ordained women. Sex is still the dangerous realm of dark powerful forces especially embodied in woman's mysterious sexuality and childbirth. But instead of new life, sex brings death. To overcome death the body processes must be severely suppressed. Sexual differences and sexual drive arise from the discredited flesh; the influence of social and cultural conditions is ignored. Masculinity and femininity are vague qualities abstracted from the male and female role in coitus. Males penetrate, females are penetrated; ergo masculinity is innately active, femininity is innately passive. Unfortunately, it is almost as if the biological basis of the argument rests on a residue of the ancient and medieval belief that masculine sperm provided all the creative potential for forming the new child, while the female's only contribution was inert blood and womb. The active

sperm created the new man using female matter, and if conditions were unfavorable—if say a strong moist south wind
was blowing—then development would be retarded and a
female (or misbegotten male) would be born. It gives one
pause. If the discovery of the female ovum had not come as
late as 1880, would the identification of masculinity and active creativity have been so thoroughly entrenched in
Catholic tradition?

Such a strong negative distortion of Christian thought was
bound to produce a reaction. In recent times, many champions have arisen to do battle against the negative Catholic
tradition regarding sex and femininity. Their aim is to re-
deem sexuality, and ransom femininity from its degraded
state. Sex they insist is not "the focal point of sin," but rather
a road to salvation. The physical procreation of the sexes
mirrors the spiritual effects of "creative encounter with the
complementary sex."[34] Reciprocal relationships between the
sexes are physically and spiritually fruitful; children, creative
love, unity, and sanctification result. All creativity, culture
and progress are the results of the exercise and interplay of
this most divine gift to man. It is even postulated that human
sexuality somehow reflects Divinity. God made mankind in
his own image, male and female, and the giving, loving, and
fruitful union of human sexuality reflects the Trinity's relationships. The duality and unity of man and woman is "the
great mystery, the copy of that essential fruitfulness which
has its source in the *Logos* and the Spirit, and also the model
of the generous love of the Trinity."[35] Sex is not only the
essence of "those polar forces which govern the universe,"[36]
but symbolizes the union of God and man. Much is made of
the sexual symbols in Scripture: God is faithful husband to
Israel, Christ is the bridegroom of the Church, and each soul
must be a bride in the Spirit.

Usually, it is the Spirit which is identified as the feminine element in the Godhead. Sophisticated defenders of sexuality and femininity hasten to point out that Syriac Fathers, in whose language "Spirit" was feminine, went so far as to call it our Mother. They maintain that even among the patriarchal Hebrews there was some concept of the Spirit as feminine. After all, God speaking through Isaias says, "Shall not I that make others to bring forth children, myself bring forth . . ." and "As one whom the mother caresseth, so will I comfort you . . ." (Isaias 66:9,13). God is not just "Father," but "Mother," too. Sex and femininity are no longer the flawed consequences of creaturedom, but reflect the Creator of the universe.

But within all the new interpretations given sex, masculinity and femininity remain opposites; they are reconciled only in God. Masculinity is still defined as mind, act, aggressiveness, rationality, and penetration—and hence opposed to feminine receptivity, passive expectancy, nurturing, intuition, and so on. Woman must still find her fulfillment in "responsive self-surrender, her conceiving in love . . . her patience . . . her motherliness and protectiveness."[37] All souls are feminine to God, but women, naturally more spiritual, must exemplify the "Eternal Feminine" and lead the world back to God—Beatrice, Mary, the New Eve. Polarization of the sexes is still all-important. It is vital that "the receptivity and protectiveness of the mother is combined with the procreativity and creativity of the man."[38] Men and women are incomplete without a polarized and complementary relationship to the opposite sex. "The man needs the woman for the most complete development of his manhood . . ." and woman reaches "the most profound level of her femininity, her womanhood and her maternity in her contact with the man."[39] Man in possession of the "giving fertilizing factor,"[40]

must enact "predominantly the creative and generative principle," while woman is "predominantly the receptive principle in relation to man."[41] (Shades of the old assumptions of
masculine superiority.)

In other words, although sex and femininity are glorified,
men and women are confined to the same hackneyed stereotypes of masculinity and femininity as in the most pessimistic
anti-feminine tradition. Sexual differences are still considered a "metaphysical, as well as a physical and cultural distinction."[42] There are still masculine souls and feminine
souls: the physical difference is the indication of the difference of soul. Different souls, and metaphysical differences between men and women still impose different vocations in the
world. Feminine souls (and women) are meant for hidden
contemplation; so their more spiritual nature should now
willingly accept segregated subordination as the better part.
Women therefore are shuffled willy-nilly into vocations as
"the heart" of this or that—and limited and discriminated
against as much as ever. Sex is glorified, woman is glorified,
but sexual differences (reflecting the Divinity) make the
world go round: "Man and woman are opposed to one another—in the fullness of their being, in body, mind and
soul."[43]

Can such a romantic, exaggerated view of sex be attributed
solely to violent reactions to the old pessimisms and taboos?
In part, yes. False attitudes had to be corrected and perhaps
an exaggerated enthusiasm for sex and womanhood was the
only antidote to such an ingrained suspicion of the body. A
neurotic suppression of sex very naturally creates a fevered
endorsement in reaction. In the reaction women, so involved
in sexual functioning, soared from carnal depths to spiritual
heights, simply by virtue of their womanhood—just as for
marriage and sexual intercourse the same transformation

takes place. What used to be a temporal concession to lust and procreation is now an existential encounter of love mirroring divinity and heaven; sex in itself and by itself has now become sacred.

Optimism has so carried the day that an avant-garde Jesuit could reply to a lady troubled "that in heaven there will be no marriage" with the assurance that, "in heaven, dear madam, there will be absolute promiscuity, ab-so-lute promiscuity." Sexual mysticism is almost party line to be duly mass-produced and disseminated. Avant-garde Christian circles practice their own sexual one-upmanship, with the Song of Songs enjoying a revival and Christian celibacy considered a neurotic anachronism. If Christians are being attacked on their sexual ethic of restraint from all sides, they must now prove that they are as pro-sex as everybody else.

And there is no denying that at the moment, everybody else is very pro-sex. A debased Freudianism reigns in popular culture and "the sexual sell" is in full swing. The axiom is simple: sexual drives, or their repression, motivate man's actions and sexual fulfillment is his goal. Anyone who has soured on this popular axiom speaks very softly. When Betty Friedan protests against the sexual sell to women in her book *The Feminine Mystique,* she covers her attack by statistics showing that women who do not live for sex alone have better sex than anybody.[44] In other studies the frequency of orgasms is duly tabulated among different religious groups.[45] A culture obsessed enough by sexuality to make such surveys has certainly pressured a Christian reaction which competes with its own sexual mystique.

The Christian sexual mystique has been built up on the vast differences that science has supposedly "proved" between men and women. Having discovered female ova, hormones, and fat tissue, thinkers have catalogued and em-

braced these innate differences. Certain psychiatric theories
are further adduced as proof; after all, Freud maintained of
women that her anatomy is her destiny. Penis envy has dire
effects, and childbirth determines women to passive expectancy and nurturing functions. Furthermore, quasi-symbolic
scientific deductions are still made from the physical process
of coitus. Big placid female ova are penetrated by fast-swim-
ming torpedo sperms, so that femininity is placid—passive—
while masculinity is active penetration. But this mystical
view of sex (like its secular counterpart discussed in Chapter
I) also rests on shaky scientific grounds. There is as yet no
scientific proof that the different reproductive functions affect the personality apart from environmental and cultural
influences. So far male and female distinctions must be re-
stricted to different sexual organs, different physiques, with
big question marks remaining about the influence of heredity and hormones.

The preliminary conclusions of Chapter I hold true for
Christian thinkers too. For what all the romanticizers and
exaggerators of sex have underrated is the finding of the rising social sciences. Social analysis has shown that any group
denied rights, initiative, education, and leadership becomes
of necessity passive, dependent, intuitive, and emotional.
These innate "spiritual" attributes have a way of disappear-
ing with the advent of equality, as shown in the case of the
American Negro. It is necessity, not nature, that has made
women seek satisfaction in personal and concrete concerns
rather than in aggressive abstract thought. "The eyes of the
handmaid are on the hand of her mistress" because the handmaid's welfare depends on the personal satisfaction she gives.
The weak become adept at personal relations because they
have to. Humility, too, can be imposed from without. Many
of the oppressed groups throughout history "have known

their place," and even agreed with the justifications of privilege propounded by the powerful. It is more and more apparent that social conditioning in matters sexual is all-important. Even the innermost psychic development of a self-image can be molded by environment. As for Freud's psychoanalytical interpretation of woman's handicaps, it too has now been seriously questioned on the basis of Freud's limited experience and his personal conditioning in his masculine-dominated society. Woman's "anatomy is destiny" if society insists upon it, but a study of different cultures shows that the sexual differences can be either minimized or exaggerated.

Indeed, the innate biological functioning of the body seems less simple all the time. The problems involved in psychosomatic medicine complicate the relations of physical differences and mental states. The findings in genetics, which at first so supported the "different in every cell" approach, are uncovering new complications in sexual differentiation. If there are sexual mosaics, which are both male and female and have both male and female cells, what becomes of the assumed inexorable divisions into male and female? It is well to remember that a scientist like Julian Huxley can say: "Sex itself is illuminated by our genetic knowledge. In origin it has nothing to do with sexual differentiation, the difference between males and females of a species; its basic and universal function is to provide the species with greater genetic variability."[46]

Christian writers dealing with sex must become more aware of the uncertainties of science, and reappraise their glib assertions that since body and soul are one, therefore there are masculine souls and feminine souls. What about the hermaphrodite, sexual mosaic, or even the "eunuch from his mother's womb"? Do inherited psychological and physical deformities indicate misshapen souls? The relation between psyche, body and soul is a complex and delicate one. In the battle against gnosticism and the false idea of the soul imprisoned in the body, have not many Christians, especially Catholics, become too *simpliste*, static, materialistic in their emphasis? Biological and sex differences are emphasized more than other individual differences. Would not the individual differences between a Pigmy male and a female Russian athlete be more determinative than their sexual differences? Then again, the changing phases of the body from infancy to old age are ignored, and attention is drawn to the reproductive period. Of course, the real default in the discussion is that there is not enough Christian thinking being done about the human body and its destiny. As Karl Rahner says, theologians have avoided thinking about the profound implications of the Resurrection of the Body. Moreover, St. Paul's words about the body "being for the Lord," and sown as a seed to give rise to a spiritual body also need explication and development. It is important to know God's plan for eternity in order to decide the temporal importance of sexual differences, or any other physical differences for that matter. How and why was Christ so different in appearance that neither the disciples nor Mary Magdalene could recognize Him immediately?

Faced with the mysterious and unknown, it is rash for Christians to build superstructures of sexual theories based only upon assertions that sexual differences are somehow "metaphysical." It is both bad science and bad theology when Christians approvingly quote Nietzsche's assertion that sexuality in the person extends "from the physical roots to the spiritual crown of the tree of life."[47] Bad philosophy is also involved, say some new defenders of feminine equality. Using St. Thomas' philosophy against himself, they conclude

that when Thomas claimed human reason and will independent of matter, he contradicted his justification of feminine subordination. Woman's equality and full humanity
follow the Thomistic thesis that the soul is "an immaterial
reality created by God." Thus, what is fundamental in man
as a human being—his reason and his will—is independent of
physiological structure.[48] It follows therefore that "within an
authentically Thomistic context, the only nature woman has
is *human* nature."[49] So much, then, for Nietzsche's thesis and
the "metaphysical" differences of men and women.

Romantic speculations about sexuality in the Divinity
seem even farther astray. Indeed, it is to renounce the great
revelation to the Hebrews, who surrounded by gods and god-
desses, insisted that God, "He who is," was above and beyond
sexual differences. In contrast to the divine couples of the
Semitic world, the person of God is completely severed from
sexuality: "God is unique, which means that He is not like
man, nor woman, nor both of them together."[50] God is the
creator, not the procreator, and He freely introduced sexuality into the creation. Attempts to prove that "male and
female created in His image" reflect the Trinity always fall
apart upon the rocks of theological truths. The vague analogies sound good until faced with the unity and uniqueness
of Divinity; attributing femininity to the Spirit or to the Son
just won't work. Whatever the correct understanding of the
analogy of God to man, sexual differences (like racial differences) are superseded.

It makes more sense to follow St. Gregory of Nyssa when
he writes that "the whole of human nature, from the first
man to the last, is but one image of Him who is. The division into male and female was something superadded to the
work of creation."[51] A good "something," but not as important as romantics maintain. Furthermore, when Christ be-

came man (*anthropos*), although specifically masculine (*aner*) and Jewish, he redeemed all mankind. One scholar proves this point by noting that "the Epistles, when speaking of the work of Jesus Christ, always carefully speak of him as 'anthropos' (or man in the general sense of a human being)."[52] Christ the new Man into whom all Christians are to grow embodies the fullness of humanity in which masculinity and Jewishness are incidental.

Nor does the frequent use of sexual images in Scripture and mystical writings contradict the view that sexual differences are a superadded aspect of creation that do not mirror Divinity. Naturally men used familiar patriarchal analogies to express the divine mystery. God as the faithful husband to whoring Israel, Christ as the bridegroom come to the wedding—nuptial images express well mutual love and commitment. But it is unwise to overemphasize the sexual images. They must take their place alongside all the other images used to express the relationship between man and God. In Old Testament imagery God is also called King, Judge, General, Father, Mother (more rarely), consuming fire; Christ besides bridegroom is also King, Judge, good shepherd, brother, friend, Lamb, Vine, and Bread of Life. The mystery of loving union with diversity is well expressed by other than sexual symbols.

Perhaps earlier mystics overworked the sexual symbols of Christianity in reaction to the prevailing ascetic repression and degrading of sex. When sexuality was wrongly identified with "the flesh" against which the Spirit must war, then all sexual drive and expression had to be translated into spiritual terms and projected into eternity. Now that scriptural scholarship has shown that St. Paul's use of "flesh" included all of man's faculties when not directed by the Spirit, the over-emphasis upon the body's dangers can be corrected. Karl

Rahner observes that it is more often the rational and intellectual faculties of man which lead him into sin, rather than any rebellion of the body.[53] Celibacy may be a difficult sacrifice to make, but obedience and poverty are as demanding if not more so. At any rate, celibacy is no longer advocated because of the intrinsic evil of sexuality, but because the sacrifice of such a high good of creation (partaking of the foolishness of the Cross) witnesses to the new world of eternity, and can free the person for more inclusive love and service. Celibacy, like poverty and obedience, is meritorious only "for the sake of the kingdom," for the use of sexuality can be sanctified like any other good gift of God. This will be more clear when some married saint is canonized who did not bury or leave his or her spouse, but lived a long and happily married life.

Sexuality, then, is neither a focus of sin nor by itself a sacred reflection of the Divine. It is a high and central good of creation, but not the mainspring of the universe. Sexual identity, or sexual encounter, is not of itself more creative or valuable than any other. Marc Oraison is right when he says that, "The paradox of sexuality consists in the fact that it is one of the most intense of the psycho-emotional powers, but that in the spiritual synthesis of the personality it is of only secondary importance."[54] It is of secondary importance because as Oraison goes on to say, "it is only a register of the manifestations of the personality."[55] The whole personality is of primary importance. Sexual identity and sexual expression are only aspects of the personality, which must be sanctified. Of itself, sex neither hinders nor helps in the new life. Sexuality is, perhaps, a pre-language, a direct non-reflective language, which (like the gift of tongues) can be directed to the praise of God as well as for communion with others. As with speech, almost everything depends upon the intention of

man in his heart and the conformity of heart and deed. As
St. Paul says: "whether you eat or drink, whatever you do,
do for the glory of God."

But when the glory of God is all in all, what of sexuality?
The pessimists seem very wrong to visualize heaven as sexless
because of the connection between sex and death; but are the
enthusiasts right in equating the ecstasy of union with God,
with the ecstasy of sexual union? Christ said that in heaven
there would be no marriage, but all would be as the angels.
The problem then is in what way will mankind's distinct,
glorified and bodily life resemble angelic life? The best
guess, perhaps, is closer to the optimists: temporal sexuality
is a pale reflection of the communal joy of heaven, but only
one part of that joy. Knowing may be as great a joy as the
giving and receiving of love. Every human aspiration and
faculty, including sexuality, will be fulfilled, but there may
be no marriage because marriage involves a temporal focus
upon one person, impossible when all limitations of time are
transcended. Since human procreation, too, takes place in
time, the procreation of marriage could also be superseded.
In the kingdom of heaven there should only be the joy of the
new child, and none of the temporal travail and incomplete
longing for a new birth. In the eternal Now, the joy and
communion of the individual with the rest of the Mystical
Body and Christ might well supersede the exclusive union
of marriage.

Nor would the communion of heaven be compatible with
any "metaphysical" divisions of the sexes. Sex, like class and
race, should not be a principle of division in heaven: in
Christ there is neither Jew or Greek, slave or free, male or
female. These more superficial distinctions of humanity may
remain as testimony of the Divine delight in variety, but the
unity and loving communion of all with all would be the

important thing. Ultimately, after reviewing all of Scripture without cultural bias, the truest Christian view of sexuality is that it is created by God specifically for procreation and generally (along with all other differences between persons) for the expression of love and the creation of unity from diversity. Certainly woman's only specific sexual role (if she freely chooses marriage) is the physical carrying and bearing of children. Any limitations or discrimination other than purely physical or procreative ones is the un-Christian result of bad theology based upon false scientific and cultural assumptions. Vocations within the body of Christ may differ according to individual gifts, but the gifts do not come with sexual labels. The Spirit bloweth where it listeth, and woe to those who impose arbitrary boundaries to Christian liberty.

The Christian ideal is that the human person "grow up into the fullness of Christ." It was a good thing when Christians were denounced for destroying sexual distinctions; this is as it should be. If there is such a thing as innate sexual characteristics of personality (which seems doubtful), then Christians should strive to go beyond them by incorporating and cultivating the opposite qualities too. The Church has preached this for centuries to men: Christian men have been told that every soul must be "feminine" to God. Men have struggled to curb "masculine" aggression and self-assertion, and cultivate love and service to others. But women have been told that they have a spiritual head start, and that they should intensify their "feminine" passivity and acquiescence. As a result of such a one-sided spirituality, many Christians withdrew too much from the world, and in following a false idea of "feminine" obedience and humility, abdicated their responsibility to subdue the world and make all things new in Christ. Christians must now be wakened to the call to the freedom, activity, and apostolate of the sons of God. Woman, especially, must be shaken from her retreat into passivity; she too is called to be a son of God, to struggle and to initiate the Lord's work. In traditional sexual imagery every Christian is to be both bride echoing the Spirit's "Come," and at the same time, son. "He who overcomes shall possess these things, and I will be his God, and he shall be my son" (Apoc. 21,7). Women who are to "overcome" can engage in aggressive effort, active leadership (even over men if need be), and rational, abstract work in the world. Individual vocation and the needs of a particular situation will determine whether aggressive action or passive acceptance is appropriate Christian behavior; sexual difference should have little to do with it. Christian charity will always urge that no one needlessly scandalize others, or show superfluous scorn for one's own culture; but Christian freedom is also a freedom from culturally imposed stereotypes. The Christian ideal imposes the fullness of humanity upon each individual. When each individual seeks fullness and perfection, then no individual talent can be sacrificed to sexual role; the whole human community benefits when individuals are free to grow.

Many a great feminine saint has built up the Church and the community by her "unfeminine" behavior. The astounding Catherine of Siena touched upon this very problem in her diary. She records that she complained to the Lord that she could not do His bidding since her sex was an obstacle. But the Lord only answered: "I pour out my Spirit upon whomsoever I will. There is neither man nor woman, plebeian or noble. All are equal in my sight. . . . Therefore, my daughter, it is my will that you should appear in public."[56] Catherine appeared in public, as did other great Christian women—all undaunted by custom. But no woman so specifically followed a vocation in defiance of culture as did Joan of Arc. She followed her Voices and displayed aggressive courage and skill in a traditionally masculine role. Not since Deborah had a woman been commanded by God to lead men into war. Furthermore, she cut her hair and claimed that her Voices instructed her to wear male clothing until her mission was accomplished. The contemporary churchmen who tried her were outraged by behavior so "scandalous to womanly modesty" and contrary to the "virtue of women."[57] Whole portions of the accusations against Joan concerned the fact that she "walked with men without shame," and "against the bidding of God and His saints, she proudly and presumptuously assumed domination over men."[58]

History has of course judged who was proud and presumptuous; Joan was a martyr to masculine arrogance as well as political intrigue. True to her conscience, she adhered to Christ and her personal vocation until death. St. Joan can be both portent and patroness of this new age of the Church when Christian women will also grow up and enter into the fullness of Christ. May the Church invoke Joan and listen to Pope John XXIII who wrote in *Pacem in Terris*:

It is obvious to everyone that women are now taking a part in public life. This is happening more rapidly, perhaps, in nations of Christian civilization, and more slowly, but broadly, among peoples who have inherited other traditions or cultures. Since women are becoming ever more conscious of their human dignity, they will not tolerate being treated as mere material instruments, but demand rights befitting a human person both in domestic and public life. . . . Human beings have the right to choose freely the state of life which they prefer, and therefore the right to set up a family, with equal rights and duties for man and woman.

If it is true that we have been distorting Scripture, and mis-interpreting Eve, Mary, and science with prejudiced minds, now in a time of general reform is our opportunity to renew Christian fullness with Christian liberty.

NOTES

[1] Fernand Prat, S.J., *The Theology of St. Paul* (Westminster, Md.: Newman, 1926) , Vol. I, p. 121.

[2] Quoted by Sister Teresa Margaret, D.C., in "Edith Stein; Woman's Role in Germany Between the Wars," *The Tablet* (London) , CCXVII (August 10, 1963) , p. 862.

[3] John Milton, *Paradise Lost,* Book IV, lines 441, 1638.

[4] Quoted by Derrick Sherwin Bailey in *The Man-Woman Relation in Christian Thought* (London: Longmans, Green & Co., 1959) , p. 64.

[5] Jean Mouroux, *The Meaning of Man* (New York: Sheed & Ward, 1948) , p. 223. The Mouroux statement is quoted approvingly by John Fitzsimons in *Woman Today* (New York: Sheed & Ward, 1952) , p. 173.

[6] Fitzsimons, *op. cit.,* p. 87.

[7] F. X. Arnold, *Woman and Man* (New York: Herder & Herder, 1963) , p. 21.

[8] *Ibid.,* p. 148.

[9] Quoted by Carroll Camden, *The Elizabethan Woman* (Houston: Elsevier Press, 1952) , p. 18.

[10] Cf. Theodore Reik, *The Creation of Woman* (New York: Braziller, 1960) .

[11] Address to the Montreal Medical Association reported in *Search,* Vol. II (August, 1963) , p. 136.

[12] *Ibid.,* p. 137.

[13] Pastor André Dumas, *Biblical Anthropology and the Participation of Women in the Ministry of the Church* (Geneva: World Council of Churches, 1963) , p. 20.

[14] *Paradise Lost,* Book IX, lines 906-907.

[15] Quoted by Pastor Dumas, *op. cit.,* p. 22.

[16] John L. McKenzie, S.J., *The Two-Edged Sword* (Milwaukee: Bruce, 1956) , p. 95.

[17] Karl Rahner, S.J., *Theological Investigations* (Baltimore: Helicon, 1961) , Vol. I, p. 267.

[18] Marc Oraison, *Love or Constraint?* (New York: Paulist Press, 1961), p. 130.

[19] Arnold, *op. cit.,* p. 58.

[20] *Ibid.,* p. 62.

[21] *Ibid.,* p. 56.

[22] Ben F. Meyer, S.J., "But Mary Kept All These Things . . ." *The Catholic Biblical Quarterly,* XXVI (Jan., 1964), p. 43.

[23] Jean Guitton, *Essay on Human Love* (London: Rockliff, 1951), p. 97.

[24] Pierre Grelot, *Man and Wife in Scripture* (New York: Herder & Herder, 1964), p. 71.

[25] Jean Guitton, *op. cit.,* p. 97.

[26] *Ibid.,* p. 95.

[27] *Ibid.,* p. 96 (the "we" reveals this as a masculine approach).

[28] Fitzsimons, *op. cit.,* p. 186.

[29] *Ibid.,* p. 187.

[30] Louis Bouyer, *The Seat of Wisdom* (New York: Pantheon, 1962), p. 87.

[31] *Ibid.*

[32] *Ibid.,* p. 94.

[33] *Ibid.,* p. 189.

[34] Bailey, *op. cit.,* p. 286.

[35] Arnold, *op. cit.,* p. 18.

[36] *Ibid.,* p. 15.

[37] *Ibid.,* p. 14.

[38] *Ibid.,* p. 15.

[39] *Ibid.,* p. 16.

[40] Dietrich von Hildebrand, *In Defense of Purity* (Baltimore: Helicon, 1962), p. 188.

[41] *Ibid.*

[42] Bailey, *op. cit.,* p. 288.

[43] Arnold, *op. cit.,* p. 98.

[44] Betty Friedan, *The Feminine Mystique* (New York: W. W. Norton, 1963), p. 327.

[45] Michael Argyle, *Religious Behaviour* (London: Routledge & Kegan Paul, 1958), p. 121.

[46] Julian Huxley, "Evolution and Genetics," *What is Science?* ed. James R. Newman (New York: Washington Square Press, 1961), p. 285.

[47] Quoted by Arnold, *op. cit.,* p. 98.

[48] Gertrude Heinzelmann, "Petition to Preparatory Commission of the Vatican Council" (Adapted by Rosemary Lauer) *The Catholic Messenger* (Davenport, Iowa), July 2, 1964, p. 5.

[49] Rosemary Lauer, "Women and the Church," *The Commonweal*, Vol. LXXIX (December 20, 1963), p. 366.

[50] Pastor Dumas, *op. cit.*, p. 12.

[51] Quoted by Father de Lubac, S.J., *Catholicism* (New York: Sheed & Ward, 1958) pp. 5 and 211.

[52] Pastor Dumas, *op. cit.*, p. 13.

[53] Karl Rahner, S.J., "Theological Concept of Concupiscentia," *Theological Investigations* (Baltimore: Helicon, 1961), Vol. I, p. 355.

[54] Oraison, *op. cit.*, p. 136.

[55] *Ibid.*

[56] Quoted by Pastor Dumas, *op. cit.*, p. 22.

[57] John Beevers, *St. Joan of Arc* (New York: Doubleday, 1962), p. 113.

[58] *Ibid.*

FOUR

Woman as Wife:
the Man-Woman Relationship

Developing a new theoretical approach to women is one thing, living it another. Even after arguments for woman's equality and freedom have been accepted, the challenge of applying them in the modern world remains. Undoubtedly, the new ideal of initiative and "growing up in Christ" will be easiest for the single woman to achieve. Already the culture expects the single woman to have a serious commitment to her vocation and to be responsible and active as well as traditionally feminine. She faces no conflicts with husband and family life as she strives for true Christian maturity and enlarged responsibilities. But the case of the married woman is very different. She must grow beyond one-sided sexual stereotypes, while at the same time living with a husband and engaging in the one certain "feminine" activity, childbearing. What is needed at present is a developed outline for a new husband-wife relationship that incorporated the best values of the old tradition, while welcoming new developments.

As a beginning, the latent Christian tradition of mutuality and equality in marriage should be stressed. Following St. Paul, the Church has always maintained the equal rights of the spouses over the other's body; but now the equal and

mutual rights to love, care and psychological union must also
be asserted. Married relationships too have benefited from
the whole recent Christian movement to restore the inner
spiritual dimension to a juridical framework. Now a woman's equal right to the marriage act and her equal immunity
from being "put away" is but the bare legal bones of the
ideal of the unity of equals. Husband and wife today must
love one another and mutually achieve the organic unity of
one-fleshness at every level of their relationship—"that the
two may become one." St. Paul told the married to "be subject to one another" and love and sacrifice for one another as
Christ loved and gave Himself to the Church. Spiritual communion, mutual sanctification, emotional and physical fulfillment—for these Christians marry. "Rights" and "ends"
become psychologically irrelevant, mere letters of the law,
when love's unity matures.

When a one-sided juridical approach to marriage is found
inadequate, the traditional idea of the husband as the "head
of the wife" and "head" of the family is also untenable. For
one thing, the scriptural texts concerning the husband as
"head" (discussed in Chapter 2) are too uncertain to support
the weight of traditional masculine authority. More and
more it becomes clear that it has been the practice of patriarchy rather than a developed Christian theology which has
enthroned the husband as "head." Theologians living in patriarchal, hierarchal societies have assumed that every society
must have "a head." In the miniature society of marriage the
husband was to be that "head" since he already participated
in the general masculine superiority and privilege granted
by God. This static world consisted of great hierarchical
chains, and whether one started from the Pope as head of the
Church or the Emperor as head of the State, wives would be
found far, far down the chain of command.

The Church always recognized, of course, that in exceptional cases some wives would have to assume authority. If the husband died, or failed in his duty to support the family, or was too immoral to guide it, then the wife was obligated to take over the husband's place. In reality, the father's authority and duties were decidedly more functional than inherent. Indeed, Fathers John Ford, S.J., and Gerald Kelly, S.J., in their important book on marriage questions, specifically deny the charge of Reinhold Niebuhr that in Catholicism the husband's domination is an absolute. "The natural law . . ." they say, "requires the headship of the father, not as an absolute, but as the normal."[1] There is no recourse to an absolute standard drawn from revelation, but only a reliance on "normality." And in times past it was normal for the father to head the family. Women were not educated or allowed equal opportunities in the world. They could hardly support a family, or have the experience necessary for judgments about the family welfare. Furthermore, childbearing without much medical knowledge was an arduous, dangerous, and often debilitating experience. Without any control of fertility and with an earlier death, a woman could well be pregnant or nursing all of her adult life. Even without external dangers in lawless times, the normal woman required the support, care, protection and guidance of a husband. It is no wonder that one-way pledges of obedience were a part of the marriage service and inexactly equated with the religious vow of obedience.

But now the world has changed and with it what is "normal." Women are equally educated, equal under the law, have equal opportunity (almost) for employment, and with the aid of medicine equally good health. A moral control of fertility is now available and justified by our urbanized, industrialized, crowded world. But even if a woman continues childbearing until menopause, she can still look forward to twenty more years of life and the likely prospect that she will outlive her husband. But even more important, this new feminine life-pattern is lived within a dynamic, mobile society imbued with the democratic (and Christian) values of equality and liberty. Static, rigidly structured societies with a head and hierarchy have almost disappeared. When crowned "heads" are rare, women preside at the UN or orbit the earth, and the Pope himself accepts the concept of collegiality, the "normal" can no longer justify the husband as head of the wife.

An indication of how things are going is found in the fact that whole books on Catholic marriage are now written without reference to the husband as head of the family. Only mutual love and responsibility are mentioned. In the more popular, less intellectual books, where the husband is still declared the head of the family, the writers all take pains to show that the modern husband must exercise his greater authority by greater service, sacrifice, and responsibility for the happiness of all his family. Only infrequently need he exercise his paternal authority as naked authority; but on those rare occasions when no agreement can be reached, the husband as head must make the final decision. The corollary implication is clear: in conflicts, the wife must submit her judgment and conscience to her husband and obey him. Again, the rationale for this is no longer theological, but simply the fixed idea that in every society, however small, anarchy will result unless one person has authority to decide conflicts and ensure efficient operation. This reasoning sounds sensible, but does it really work?

Perhaps such systems operated in places and times when people were less sensitive to justice; but our common-law tradition takes a dim view of empowering one of two disputants to decide his own case. Star chamber procedures may make for efficiency in the short run, but ultimately free juries and the consent of the governed do better. As for the intimate union of marriage, mutual consent and agreement are even more important. Marriage today is not a society like other societies. It is more like being alone together on a raft, or survival on a desert isle; there is no support from an ordered milieu wherein some things are certain and taken for granted. In this kind of isolated, mobile, fluctuating relationship, when one eats, sleeps and works with another and depends upon him or her for emotional satisfaction, the only way to operate is by pure democracy. Both can agree to follow the decision of the one who knows most about a particular activity, but neither one can always have the final say about everything.

A loving marriage today is just too intimate a relationship for lines of command or a hierarchy to exist. Two mature people cannot affirm that the husband, solely because he is a male, ought to decide finally disputed questions. The more important the decision, the less one can submit a dissenting judgment or a reserved conscience to another's arbitrary decision. In desperate cases husband and wife can agree to submit to the judgment of a third party, but generally prayerful reasoning together in love should be the way to a solution. Within marriage the aim of "being in one mind with Christ" is fulfilled by waiting together upon the Spirit, not by arbitrary submission of one person to another. Christians can now outgrow a pagan patriarchy and Christian marriage can live up to its own highest ideals of love. For "lovers," in the words of a Catholic psychiatrist, "do not tend, either consciously or unconsciously, to subjugate the other person . . . they aspire to realize a communion between two equalities, as being of the very essence of love."[2]

Furthermore, in a fully Christian restoration of a loving, one-flesh unity and equality in marriage, I believe that the traditional division of sexual roles and identities must also be transcended. Traditionally, man was assigned primacy in governing, and woman "primacy in loving," as the "head" and "heart" of the home respectively. But this idea seems an inadequate expression of the injunction to Christians to "grow up into the fullness of Christ." Christian fullness and maturity should include the fullest development of *both* governing and loving by *both* husband and wife. Husband and wife should strive for completeness, to be both head and heart simultaneously. Surely no Christian man pledged to imitate Christ can concede "primacy of loving" (whatever this means) to another. In fact, no aspect of human perfection can be relegated to the partner-parent of the other sex. Even if innate sexual dispositions or cultural formation makes it more difficult to love or govern, nonetheless compensatory efforts to develop and exercise the opposite qualities and functions must be made. "Putting on Christ" will mean imitating "the perfect One" who loves and governs with all wisdom and tenderness. The Jesus who laments that He would gather the people of Jerusalem Himself as a mother hen gathers her chicks, also drives the money changers from the Temple. He is the fullness and perfection of humanity and bids us all to follow Him.

Yes, in persuading husbands and wives to imitate Christ in the same ways, I am arguing for an androgynous (male-female) ideal for married Christians. Husbands and wives should be striving for the same goal of personality. This goal would be the integration in each person of the active-passive Christian virtues traditionally apportioned out to the two sexes. The point of this apportioning was mainly to ensure a complementary relationship between husband and wife—ac-

tive husband complemented by predominantly passive wife
—but I think this is a confining idea of complementary relationships. Husband and wife can complement each other,
but they do not exist in a total vacuum but within the communion of the Church, the whole body of which they must
also complement. The husband and wife's individual role in
the community of the Church and world should affect the
way they complement one another. Complementing one another should be a matter of individual talents and competen-
cies compensating for the other's needs and inadequacies on
the road to perfection and fullness. In other words, every
husband and wife do not form a microcosm of the whole human race with active and passive vocations apportioned between them. Instead, each of the married pair seeks full
individual perfection and unity, while complementing the
greater community.

To use the Pauline metaphor of the mystical body (and it
is a metaphor which should be used sparingly) a husband
and a wife might both be "eyes," or "hands," or "feet," while
seeking to grow up into Christ, the head of all. Both husband
and wife may have vocations to serve Christ in active roles of
authority in the world, or they may both serve in a hidden
contemplative vocation—or they may have different combinations of talents, gifts, and callings. The important point here
is that similar vocations do not necessarily mean unhealthy
competition between husband and wife. Similar roles can
mean a closer cooperation. The fact that two people do the
same work is a neutral fact; it is the attitude of the people
that determine whether they are competing or cooperating.
A Christian husband and wife will rule out all competition
except that of charity; each person has his gifts from God,
but the most important of these is charity.

Indeed, encouraging the sexes to be more alike can intensify married love and promote mutual sanctification. Opposites *may* attract, but in the long-term life of married love, the more in common the better. Mutual understanding is so much easier when ideas, ideals, experience, and emotional responses coincide. Perhaps nothing causes more suffering than the blanks and gaps in a mate's personality, those times when there is simply no response to some crucial concern of one's own. Unfortunately, the human condition will create enough of these natural incompatibilities without creating new ones by stressing sexual differences in education and cultural conditioning. A frivolous wife or an insensitive husband can be the end result of an exaggerated emphasis of our present feminine and masculine sex roles.

An inevitable and unfortunate result of cultivating sex differences is that the whole area of friendship is easily removed from marriage. The need to communicate with friends of like mind and like concerns is basic in human nature. It is interesting that in societies where very different sexual roles exclude friendship from marriage, there are also strong one-sex clubs or one-sex family gatherings. Both primitive New Guinean and Victorian papa had to have a sacrosanct male club house where he could find the friendship denied in marriage. In modern-day America, one-sex social life is most prevelant among the lower classes who may also be reflecting old country ways. In many a poor neighborhood men fill the corner saloons while the women remain at home. Mixed gatherings of married couples are rare, because husband and wife rarely go out together. Marriage is still an institutional and physical relationship only.

The mobile middle-classes do better: marriage is expected to include love and companionship as well as sex and support. This is almost a necessity, because the way to the top in a technological society will frequently mean moving about the country, far from the family or any stable group of "the boys" or "the girls." Consequently, husband and wife are de-pendent upon one another for friendship and emotional support. There are some critics who claim that these modern conditions put too much pressure upon marriage; they claim that to demand emotional fulfillment too, is unrealistic. I do not agree—especially when such realists cite the virtues of arranged marriages or point with approval to the Latin way of preserving the institution. The modern ideal of marriage may be set high, but this ideal is far closer to the Christian concept of loving unity between equals. All Christian love should ideally include friendship, particularly in the "one-flesh" unity of man and wife. Friends and lovers, husband and wife must be; and to be good friends they must be equal and basically alike.

Perhaps there is no more important key to the developing unity of a couple than creative conversation. Beyond the in-timate emotional and physical expression of love, there is a great need for the communication of language. The lifelong gift of the body to another must be accompanied by the gift of the inner person's emotions, thoughts, reactions and opin-ions. This giving is not always easy. Unfortunately, in our hectic modern life, schedules can become so crowded with duties and distractions that marital conversation may wither away. It helps not at all for husband and wife to be convey-ing vocal memoranda to each other; an exchange of direc-tives is not conversation.

In true conversation two equal persons are willing to take the time and the trouble to express their intimate thoughts and emotions, and go on to explore new intellectual hori-zons. Curiously, for some couples reared in a non-verbal cul-ture it is extremely trying to strive for verbal harmony. But whatever the emotional cost, verbal openness to one another is too essential to slight. Hearts and minds must truly meet, and meet often. Language distinguishes man from the animals, and the tongue is the bridle by which the whole body is led.

A true communion of the couple can be achieved and sustained by much reasoning together. Not only will husband and wife talk about the common concerns of the home, but also of the vast world beyond the immediate family. Creative conversation can be a stimulus to intellectual, artistic and emotional growth: a bridge between two different individual worlds and two constantly changing individuals. Perhaps the word "dialogue," although much overworked, can best describe the interchange contributing to the development of a good marriage. Two persons, fundamentally alike, equal and united in will grow up (and out toward the world) through creatively speaking together.

But won't an emphasis upon similarity and equality for husbands and wives result in a dull, sexless, undiverse society? Here one must answer the dire warnings about monotonous people's republics where everyone will wear undistinguishable grey pajamas. Such a prospect is dull indeed, but it does not necessarily follow from an androgynous ideal. It is quite possible to emphasize similar roles and characteristics and at the same time to emphasize physical differences. When only physical differences remain they can be cultivated as well as suppressed. While in the new ideal one would want a man or woman to react to a situation by voicing the same sentiments (rejoicing with those who rejoice, weeping with those who weep—i.e., whatever is Christianly appropriate), one would also be glad to emphasize the fact that women usually speak with a higher, softer voice and men with deeper tones. Moreover, clothing, hairstyles, ornaments—all can be very different simply to preserve a delightful variety in externals. As things are now, women have the better part in external expressions of personality, with much more freedom in fashion and personal style. But why should women have a monopoly on beauty and aesthetic expression? Men might rescue themselves from the sea of grey flannel by meditating upon the men of former times who combined gorgeous distinctive dress with sexual virility, and never gave the matter a second thought. The few early feminists who wore men's suits were doubly mistaken; first for not glorying in their own distinctive physical differences, and then for imitating the drab conformity of male dress.

In more important matters, the same principle of similar personalities enjoying physical differences still holds. While men can rejoice in their physical strength, women can delight in their one sure distinctive function: childbearing and nursing. There is less likely to be a rejection of the body or physical functions when no penalties or limitations are attached to them. Women can delight in their sex and welcome childbirth when it does not deny them initiative and intellectual development. Interestingly enough, the movement to restore the dignity and joy of childbirth and nursing has come from educated, emancipated women. In America it is the college-educated, intellectual women who, by and large, have welcomed natural childbirth and returned to nursing their babies. Just as the new Negro takes pride in distinctive Negroid features rather than imitating Caucasians, so intellectual active women now emphasize feminine beauty and physical differences. An example of this development can be seen in the Indian women politicians with their coiled hair, beautiful jewelry, and flowing saris. In Sweden, the claim has been made that although (or because?) men and women are given similar roles, the society is suffused with sexual emphasis.

The same possibility would arise from the studies cited by
Betty Friedan of "self-realized" women.[3] Their "masculine"
initiative, and activity freed them from the inhibitions of
their passive sisters: and they were sexually more vital and
successful. As for husbands, they apparently can be delighted
rather than castrated by wives who are active and more aggressive sexually. It does seem obvious that a mutual communion and mutual physical fulfillment is easier when
women have developed what have heretofore been considered masculine initiative and men have acquired feminine
sensitivities. The myth that intellectual active women must
deny their sexuality needs to give way to the real possibility
that equal, emancipated women may have more sexual energy and better relations with their husbands. If some psychologists are right, women's new equality, reaching into the
bedroom, benefits the psychic health of husband and wife.
Perhaps the universal idea that men far exceed women in
sexual interest stemmed from the fact that women were always tired from pregnancy and ill-health and could never
equal men's physical energy for any physical activity. In the
cases when women were kept in idle leisure, their inferior
status would inhibit all development; then the *necessity* to
please men sexually would lead to pretense of pleasure rather
than pleasure itself.

But while a Christian attitude towards physical differences
could at the same time consider them incidental and rejoice
in them as part of the variety of creation, exploiting the difference is another matter. The present practice of using sex
to sell everything from soap to political candidates is degrading. Old-fashioned lust exploits a person for personal sexual
pleasure; today lust itself is stimulated and promised as the
ultimate consumer reward. Sexual attractiveness is just another commodity; one which can be a means of power over

others. Our dreadful courtship customs and the blatant flirting countenanced in some social circles and offices have more to do with the power plays and strategies of war, than with love. When sex becomes a game one wins, then the Christian value of the person is lost. Perhaps at those gatherings where men prefer to talk to men, and women to women, it is partly because in that group the game is still played and as a game it is both exhausting and dissatisfying. Every Christian woman, single, married, emancipated or not, should vow that she will never use her charm, beauty or sex appeal to manipulate another person. It is a minor first step in personal integrity.

As for sanctification of the sexual instinct in marriage, it is more easily achieved by a man and wife who see themselves as two similar, equal persons united in love rather than "opposite" sexes. Their strong, personal union apart from their sexual identity is the best possible basis for successfully integrating sexuality in marriage. For one thing, their communication is not dependent on one mode of intercourse. When something goes wrong within the sexual relationship (or if absence or sickness necessitate abstinence) there not only remain open other channels for love and unity, but the openness to each other necessary to restore the physical communion. Since the sexual drive to oneness is at times so overpowering, yet in our fallen state governed by so many variables (fatigue, hormones, boredom), it is imperative that it be integrated within a unified relationship. Any view of "the other" as opposite or mysteriously different can threaten a balanced sexuality.

Approaching the husband or wife's sexuality as completely opposite can make of intercourse an impersonal, compartmentalized physical act. The humanity of the partners is submerged completely in their identity as a satisfaction for physical desire. The person becomes more of an object. Coitus actually becomes "a remedy for concupiscence" (horrible phrase) and like all medicines, 'tis better taken quickly with eyes shut. Any "I-Thou" dimension of sex is pretty well impossible. "Maleness," or "femaleness" swallows up identity as unique person. Naturally enough, heretofore men have been more guilty of making their partner an object. Even men of good will have simply put sex in a department of its own, removed from the rest of life. Not knowing how to sanctify such a troubling activity, they have relegated it completely to animal nature, and speak of "carnal knowledge" and "indulgence of the flesh" and such like.

At the other extreme, however, is an emphasis upon the married partner as "opposite" and "different," which is just as fatal. Here there is an attempt to spiritualize sexuality by an elaboration of its mystical qualities. This mystique, described in previous chapters, insists that one seeks completion in "the other" (shades of Plato's original bi-sexual being, split into two and seeking to be united). The married partner's opposite sexuality becomes sacred, a part of the mystery that contributes to the sanctifying effects of intercourse. But in all the emphasis upon mystery the individual person is also effectively bypassed. Ironically, the glorification of sex as the supreme I-Thou experience can serve as an escape from confronting the concrete individual.

Furthermore, glorifying the mystical communion can be a subtle way of rejecting and despising the body. Catholics writing about sex rarely condemn with old-fashioned Augustinian austerity, but the new mystique makes it very clear that one must not lose one's head. Control, control, restrained control can alone sanctify conjugal love. As one writer put it, "the goal of ever-deepening spiritualization of sexual relations . . . where at the moment of mutual orgasm both are elevated in prayer" is achieved by "ever-greater human control."[4] Similarly the philosopher Dietrich von Hildebrand, defending purity, warns of the "oppressive intoxicating breath of fleshly lust."[5] He maintains that "the profound reverence of the pure, his shrinking from all direct contemplation of sex, and his deep understanding of its function . . . never allow him to make the physical pleasure as such his object."[6] Each participant in the mystery, "fain to catch and cherish the fragrance of a being different from my own,"[7] must master the unacceptable "passionate" and "fierce" tendency of the body. The triumph of high seriousness is complete; mystical sex becomes sober, self-conscious effort. This is not so far from "remedies for concupiscence."

A more Christian approach to sexuality will avoid the alternating glorification and repulsion which is characteristic of primitive attitudes of taboo. The taboo mystery is dangerous in its "otherness"; when sex is seen as one of these taboo mysteries, then male and female otherness is both vital and dangerous. All sorts of safeguards and protective charms are needed when one gets near. Christians must first demythologize sex to sanctify it. This is only possible when the sexual partner's sexual identity is subordinated to his or her whole individual personality *and* when sexuality is fully accepted. When man and woman can view each other as fundamentally possessing the same human nature, then together they can be free to achieve a human attitude toward their sexuality. Certainly love and control will banish any animal aggression in the use of sex, but an over-spiritual mystique should not banish playfulness or passion. If the body is really a good creation of God, who provided each person with strong emotions, then the physical, even irrational, sensual side of man also has value. Certainly, emotions must be rationally channeled, but once directed they should not be controlled at all times. The sexuality of loving partners should be free to follow an inherently good physical process, unburdened by self-conscious seriousness. The very perfection of sexual intercourse requires a "letting go," a complete un-self-conscious oblation. It is as hopeless to control and *will* orgasms as it is to force sleep. The oblation of love must be for its own sake; sexuality is a language of its own; other speech or too much verbal thinking is distracting.

Such love will embrace spontaneous, emotional, uninhibited actions. Western Christians are far too suspicious of unseemly emotionalism and physical expression. Christ responded differently to the woman so lacking in restraint that she washed His feet with tears and dried them with her hair. The emotions, and their physical expression, should praise the Lord with their own mode of communication. Everything is not to be transposed into verbal, cerebral expression. The body's own vitality should not be suppressed by false ideas of dignity and decorum. King David pleased God by joyfully leaping and "dancing with all his might" naked before the Ark of the Covenant. When David's wife "despised him as a buffoon" and reproached him, her womb was closed and she was barren. Perfect love not only casts out fear, but it also casts out false pride, shame and inhibitions. Sanctified sexual love is not synonomous with continual sober control. Indeed, a husband and wife reconciled to their own humanity and sure of the like humanity of their mate can be so secure as to trust themselves to play and passion. They can offer the pure pleasure and the fierce irrational quality of physical love to God for what it is in itself—a part of the good Creation.

An emphasis on equality and likeness also aids in the mutual sanctification of both partners beyond their physical relationships. When husband and wife are thought of as fundamentally alike, there is little excuse for the un-Christian employment of "double standards." The Gospel is adamant in its demand for a single high standard of Christian behavior for both sexes, but in Christian practice an emphasis upon sexual differences breeds a toleration of double standards. The most usual form is privilege and indulgence of masculine failings. Men are still excused a multitude of sins for which women would be ostracized. Not only are sins against chastity thought more normal for the male, but mild tyranny and temper can characterize the "head" of many a Christian family. If all power tends to corrupt, the physical, economic and religious privileges granted men are not good omens. Nor would a matriarchy with women in the ascendancy be an improvement. Power would corrupt women just as readily. The fact that contraceptives have lessened the traditionally greater chastity of young women should surprise no one. Women probably could be conditioned to run concentration camps as well as men; only their powerlessness has led to the myth of their greater innate virtue.

Yet powerlessness too corrupts. If men have been corrupted by privilege, women have been apathetic and frivolous, petty and irresponsible, and acquiescent in their lot. As one of the famous kept ladies of our day was quoted as saying, women should always choose to be "pampered in a gilded cage," for essentially they are meant to be "beautiful prey." Well, beautiful prey in gilded cages or passive sweet maids behind the veil—neither image demands enough of women as human beings.

The task of "growing up into Christ" necessitates giving up all the excuses of sexual stereotypes. The demand for Christian perfection must penetrate the depths of the personality, and the fewer obstacles the better. If vanity or irresponsibility is no longer "feminine," or aggressiveness "masculine," there is that much less justification for my clinging to my faults. Nor in marriage of two mature equals will my partner see traditional sex failings as endearing. Tears, charm or lordly arrogance are no substitute for ma- turity—as my spouse will soon tell me—if communication is really free. Mutual sanctification involves a give–and–take that can be painful. One partner cannot demand and correct while the other only endures; both can make demands, con- cessions and compromises. The communion of love "implies a certain amount of aggressiveness" that will help establish "not a static harmony, but a dialectical harmony."[8] The strength of one comes to the aid of the other's weakness, and the objective judgment of another probes a secret self- indulgence. Growth requires honesty and honesty is best served by equality, that equality which informs the judgment of one's peers or the fraternal correction of religious life. The married grow best in grace when there is an open free inter- change of communication and a single standard of Christian perfection as a goal.

How much better for husband, wife and society that the married strive for a single standard—the perfection of Christ. Husbands, then, are not excused and exonerated on the basis of their less redeemable masculinity. Many a modern hus- band and father strives for a complete ideal and takes his family responsibilities seriously. He does not deny that sensi- tivity, consideration, patience are desirable masculine at- tributes. Nostalgic observers may deplore the passing of masculine prerogative and the "castration of the American male," but from a Christian viewpoint the masculine role is growing in charity. Men are coming to treat their wives as they themselves would want to be treated and giving them companionship, consideration and a helping hand with the housework and children. Moreover, modern men are increasingly less prone to dismiss religion as a feminine affair, or to ignore cultural concerns.

As work becomes less identified with certain sexes, men with heretofore "maternal" talents will be free to use them. A good sign in this direction is the increase of male elementary school teachers. A husband should not feel that his masculinity is threatened by any choice of vocation, family participation or certain kinds of apostolic activity. How encouraging it is to see men at last entering into the parent-teacher groups of their children's schools, or becoming active in apostolic lay groups.

But are wives reciprocating in their own development? Those who indict women for remaining retarded have a point; too often wives do lag behind their husbands. Since a husband is forced to make his way in the world, he may keep growing in intellect and responsibility. At the same time the culture and Christian conscience favor his development as a family man. But wives, supported and segregated, are not forced to grow or turn outward from their own immediate existence. Their narrow vision and lack of intellectual growth can easily degenerate into selfishness. It is all too easy in a suburban setting for all efforts to be concentrated on one's self, one's family and one's possessions—without any corresponding responsibility for the larger society beyond the home.

In the educated middle classes many women seem loath to take responsibility and seriously commit themselves. Unfortunately, it is still only a small minority of wives who keep the volunteer community groups, or local political parties operating. So much talent and time are simply frittered away. Far too rare is the woman who keeps a breadth of interest and a high level of intellectual activity. The repeated pleas for women to rejoin the world are well taken. Even without the stimulus of personal necessity the needs of the day should awaken women to further and more wide-ranging efforts. The world and the Church can not spare the wasted talents and capabilities of married women.

Are orthodox Christians more prone than others to the excuse that once a wife it is feminine to retreat from "masculine" concerns and responsibilities? I am afraid so. The bad theology and the anti-feminine cast of much of Church history have borne the fruit of much feminine apathy. Male-female relationships in Catholic cultures have been poor. Efforts are certainly needed to change some customary ideas and attitudes about women. First of all, Christian men, especially those that are priests and instructing others, must be prepared to grant equality and maturity to women. The subordination of women and/or their sentimental glorification must go. There is perhaps no better example of the sentimental approach than the typical Mother's Day sermon. But the reaction that would follow any suggestion to the preacher that these wonderful women become priests can also be predicted. All the avant-garde theological arguments for the priesthood of women would have little effect upon conditioned traditional attitudes. One cannot help but feel, as in the case of so many priests writing about women, that too much segregation from women has been harmful. Mothers, sisters, and rectory housekeepers do not prepare priests for friendship and cooperation with women. (Nor does the confessional overcome this handicap.) Priests will write more perceptively about women and give better marriage instructions when segregation of the sexes is not so strictly enforced in seminaries. Then women will not seem so distant and different; there can develop a recognition that individual differences preclude attributing to all women immutable feminine characteristics.

Christian husbands can do better. Living with a modern educated woman can lead to the wise statement of one husband, "Women? Women are people." Just so. The everyday life of marriage can convince one of the "sameness" of the sexes. Often marital disillusionment with the mystique of sex is interrelated with an unrealistic expectation of sexual differences. The neurotic desire to find "a magic helper" can become mixed up with the aura and attraction of the other sex. The authoritarian personality always desires to find refuge in "otherness," but the resources and strength of the other sex are no greater than our own. When one can stop looking for the idealization of an omnipotent mother or father and accept one's mate as an equal, then one is truly mature.

Companionship and mutual growth, then, must be stressed in a Christian education and formation for marriage. As the new emphasis upon "secondary ends" of marriage gains ground, there will be a new emphasis upon individual development so that the union will be a rich one. In our modern society, equality of education for women will be a necessity for a strong common bond of husband and wife. Men who are mature and secure enough to give up the psychological need for superiority will insist upon a wife who matches them intellectually. Unfortunately, many Christian men are still so traditionally oriented that they do not demand intellectual stimulation and companionship from their wives. Often these same men are distinctly uncomfortable with intelligent women and feel threatened by the outside interests of their wives. Nourished upon a self-image as "head" of the wife, many a husband views the further emancipation of women as one more example of the breakdown of the modern world.

But the new winds are gradually penetrating the Christian

subculture, as a spate of articles in the religious press attests. Wives are being urged to develop all of their talents and to take upon themselves more responsibility for the world beyond the home. The admonitions against work outside the home are abating. A few voices are raised in outright praise of the contribution a working wife can make to her marriage. The French Catholic psychiatrist, Father Ignace Lepp, expresses this new viewpoint when he says, "In order to insure that love will last as long as possible, it is indispensable that each couple in its own way (and each member of the couple in his and her own way) never give up trying to develop the richness of their personality."[9] And to this end, "women as well as men should seek self-realization elsewhere, principally in some professional activity."[10] A wife's commitment to a profession and the work of the world can be thoroughly Christian and may actually be encouraged as a positive development of Christian women. It is the natural consequence of the same freedom and growth beyond traditional sex roles that has led men to rejoin the family.

But every good argument has its drawbacks, so a few cautionary remarks must be inserted here. Frankly, husbands do have just reason to be a bit alarmed at the nature of some of the literature aimed at awakening modern women. In much of the writing on the subject there is no recognition of the husband's needs. The implication is that a woman must fulfill herself unmindful of husband and children. Simple charity would preclude such selfishness even if a married woman were not committed to the organic "one-flesh" unity of marriage. If a husband can no longer have the prerogative of unilateral decisions affecting the destiny of the family, neither can a wife seek her fulfillment on her own. Together husband and wife can decide how best to develop and exercise the talents and capabilities of each as an individual.

Nor can wives use self-fulfillment as an excuse for escaping dull duties at home. The ferment about women's need for wider vistas can produce damaging daydreams and an immature escapist mentality. The job outside the home can be falsely romanticized and glorified in the mind of a hard-pressed mother of young children. They forget or suppress the realization that jobs have their frustrations and can also be monotonous and unrewarding. Wives can also refuse to recognize the psychic pressures of constant competition and the hectic pace of the marketplace.

For that matter, how many men are perfectly fulfilled and able to establish complete self-identity in their work? The "nameless problem" of women that Betty Friedan discusses is not theirs alone; unfortunately, that "nameless problem" is called life. Narrowing down all psychic discontent to a lack of work fulfillment is misleading. Women, along with men, must know who they are apart from their work. Professional achievement will not serve as a panacea for problems, even among the elite men and women who have the intelligence, determination and energy to achieve their work goals. A fervent faith in work may serve a minority well for a limited part of a life-span, but basic spiritual values and questions will remain. It is ironic that work should become ever glorified just as our affluent society produces more leisure (but more on this in Chapter 6).

At this point in our changing society we are badly in need of a reality principle for wives. Before prescribing the perfections of the future the present situation must be assayed. If the society is still arranged so that different roles are assigned to husband and wife, and there are no maternity benefits or family grants from the state, then the husband must be the sole support of his wife and family during the child-bearing years. Since domestic help and the extended family have also disappeared, there is little alternative to the traditional family pattern for most women while their children are small. This is especially true if a woman has not planned from the beginning of her marriage to "be different" and go against tradition. Once involved in a traditional family pattern, a wife cannot simply make a quick reversal and impose tremendous sacrifices upon the rest of the family. Her husband will still be financially responsible, no matter what; and the children will continue to need tremendous amounts of care. Newly awakened wives may feel their potential is being wasted, but if they are enjoying the fruits of the traditional system, they must also be willing to pay the price. The husband's career must come first when in the economic structure the welfare of the whole family depends upon his success. Paradoxically, often only the wives of the very successful husband can afford the household help or the tuition fees to reenter the professional world outside the home.

In this time of transition many women must sacrifice their own schooling or development until after husbands (and sometimes children) are successfully launched. When a husband is well established and children are in school, women can go back to school or work and renew their commitment to outside work. This moderate solution to the problem of equal educated women is gaining ground everywhere. It still requires that wives make most of the sacrifices in the early years of marriage, but implies that husbands be willing to take their turn later on. When a wife is ready to expand her horizons, her husband should offer moral support and shoulder more homemaking tasks, or at least gracefully accept lower standards in unessentials. It may be hard for some husbands to heave to in a way their fathers, and some of their neighbors, would ridicule, but the desire to have a wife happily fulfilling herself is a strong motivation. A secure husband will be flexible and feel uncompromised by heretofore feminine tasks.

However, all husbands are not so, and myriad adjustments have to be made. A wife cannot demand change from a husband too rigid to bend (or vice versa). The reality of previous cultural formation and family backgrounds have to be taken into account. If love and persuasion won't bring a husband to housework or acceptance of a wife's outside interests, then charity and the primary commitment to one's marriage must prevail. One cannot agree with a Betty Friedan who can tolerantly comment that a wife's going to work to find her identity "perhaps precipitated the divorce, but it also made her more able to survive it."[11] Christian couples must be conscious of their "one flesh" unity; they can only seek identity *within* the context of love and commitment to another. With good will almost every incompatibility can be suffered through, but it would help if "the woman question" could be consciously considered by engaged couples. The whole question of personal talents and vocation should be thrashed out before the wedding. Disappointment, if not disaster, can result if a man cannot accept a woman's dedication to outside work, or, more rarely, wishes a high-powered colleague and gets a homebody.

The word "homebody" brings up one other side of reality which puzzles many of those calling upon women to fight for separate identities and a place in the sun. Why are so many traditional women contented with their lot? The prevailing explanation of this acquiescence in the "housewife trap" is cultural conditioning to inferiority in a "feminine mystique," i.e., a basic immaturity. This may be true in some cases, but the important point missed by so many feminists is that a woman with a mature self-identity can freely choose to sacrifice certain self-fulfillments for the sake of husband and a large family. Admittedly, Christians have overemphasized the tradition of womanly sacrifice, and in so doing have exacted the wrong sacrifices from the wrong people, but at least they have recognized and conserved a whole spiritual dimension of life totally absent from current discussions of fulfillment. "Losing one's life in order to find it" makes no sense to the secular world; women who choose a hidden life of sacrifice in the home, or worse still the convent, are viewed as neurotic seekers for martyrdom. All such sacrifice has become suspect. Love, and its desires to give oneself to husband and many children, is discounted as contributing to a husband's "infantile phantasy" or a neurotic escape into "breeding." However, when all vocations and free choices are encouraged except the traditional feminine role, a new tyranny and a new stereotype have simply replaced the old one.

The proposal that all young women be drafted and trained in "useful" occupations needed by the society is as disconcerting as the old confinement to lady-like activities. What is wanted is freedom for the individual to develop in her own way, not an exchange of rigid patterns so that every woman must now have a small family and work outside the home. Some wives will always find their fulfillment and identity in support and giving to husband and children. Helping a husband in his work and life can be a satisfying vocation for many women, and not just for diplomat wives or ministers' wives. It is important only that women have equal education and freedom of choice, so that not everyone is forced into one mold. Cultural suppression and freely chosen vocation are very different. Women with equal education and a complete human ideal can, in an equal, mutual marriage relationship, stimulate their husbands, children and social circles. They can truly enrich the world by enriching the family. It should be remembered that the leisure of modern women today can be compared to that of the Renaissance man. If culture is based upon leisure, then it may be very unwise to deprive all wives of leisure by pushing them pell-mell into useful professions. After all, the liturgical life, hospitality, charitable good works, the cultivation of the arts, all depend upon a leisured group, who might as well be women—until automation enforces more general leisure upon all.

The goal, then, is equal opportunity and an emphasis upon complete human development that will prepare women (and men) with the maturity to choose freely the role or combination of roles best suited for themselves. Along with the traditional roles (somewhat transmuted), the changing concepts of male-female characteristics and work will enlarge the field of individual choice. The new difference will be the greater variety and flexibility of marriage arrangements that will flourish. Once the fatal dichotomy of femininity and serious intellectual initiative and responsibility is overcome, more wives will find that their vocation is within a profession requiring a high level of commitment and time. Such wives will pursue long-range plans for specialization just as their husbands do: and no husband will feel threatened or begrudge his wife's development. Such couples will have much less differentiation of roles than in traditional marriages. Both will be committed to vocations in the world from the beginning, and both will share the home and family responsibilities. Their similar personality goals and common responsibility for the family will provide a unity despite separate ways in the world. Any one-sided emphasis upon the husband's career would no longer be necessary when the future support of the family would not be his sole responsibility. Instead of the wife working to put her husband through school (an innovation after the War), both might work to educate both. The rare graduate school couples who now alternate their professional schooling so that both can work later are auguries of the future. Now the tremendous sacrifices exacted by such a regime discourage many who might really have such a vocation. If the future provides social and financial aid to ease the struggle, and the struggle itself becomes socially acceptable, it won't require such pioneer fortitude to combine roles. Variety and individual flexibility will replace the timeworn limitations. A Christian freedom of vocation will have conquered.

Yes, say the critics, such a goal is all very nice in theory, but what about the children? Does not parental responsibility for procreation and education of children impose all over again the traditional pattern of family life? And the traditional sex roles and characteristics? These crucial questions are so important that they require a separate chapter. Does the emancipation of woman endanger the education of children? Husbands can survive being married to the new woman (and yes, even like it better too), but the question of arrangements for childrearing is a more pressing and crucial one. What of Christian woman in her role as mother?

NOTES

[1] John C. Ford, S.J. and Gerald Kelly, S.J., *Marriage Questions,* Vol. II of *Contemporary Moral Theology* (Westminster, Md.: Newman, 1963), p. 303.

[2] Ignace Lepp, *The Psychology of Loving* (Baltimore: Helicon, 1963), p. 130.

[3] Betty Friedan, *The Feminine Mystique* (New York: W. W. Norton, 1963), pp. 324, 327.

[4] Paul M. Quay, S.J., "Contraception and Conjugal Love," *Theological Studies,* XXII (March, 1961), p. 32.

[5] Dietrich von Hildebrand, *In Defense of Purity* (Baltimore: Helicon, 1962), p. 75.

6 *Ibid.*, p. 77.
7 *Ibid.*, p. 81.
8 Lepp, *op. cit.*, p. 130.
9 *Ibid.*, p. 188.
10 *Ibid.*, p. 165.
11 Friedan, *op. cit.*, p. 354.

FIVE »»»

Woman as Mother

The trouble with most of the present-day writing proposing that women take a new place in the world is the inadequate discussion of childcare. Women *will* in the end bear the children, and how are these children to be cared for if mothers stream out of the home? The central conflict turns on the extent of women's obligations to bear and care for children. I would now like to plunge into these controversial questions, to explore various possibilities for Christian family planning and childcare, and to indicate some practical solutions.

My very first axiom is an obvious one: few things on earth are more important than the child and its education. Even within a completely secular context the children's development determines the world's future; ruthless utilitarian planners in a totalitarian state will try to better the lot of their children. As for the Christian commitment to children, it was explicitly stated when Christ rebuked his disciples, embraced the children and said: "He who accepts this child for my sake, accepts me . . . for of such is the kingdom of God." The children are "of the kingdom" because of their potentiality for trust and growth; but also because they are little ones, helpless before the powerful. As one of the poor, along with slaves, women and despised races, they are a special object of Christian concern. But as usual with the helpless, it takes centuries of Christian preaching before Christian practice changes a culture. Now that slaves, women, and other races have been granted dignity, the age of the child has come. Modern consciences are outraged when children are harmed, exploited, or treated as appendages of more powerful adults. Laws have done away with child labor, and we may soon have laws to protect children who are cruelly beaten and attacked by their parents. Those who harm these "little ones" may in Christ's words "be better off with a millstone around their neck."

But while the child is helpless, he also shows forth our "wondrous humanity," ready and eager to be renewed. Wordsworth and the romantics recognized this truth when they described children as "trailing clouds of glory." Of course, Freud and the Latin Fathers of the Church also had a point: our nature is wounded and children have a blood-thirsty, original-sin side (as in *Lord of the Flies*). But all in all, children are still the first citizens of the kingdom with their passionate innate drive toward growth and love. They seek to know, to love, to grow, to master themselves and the world; with all their overwhelming potential they are different from adults. The primitive and romantic cult of the child is perhaps the best founded of all mystical superstitions. Almost any child can at certain moments resemble "the holy child." Children are important.

Once the child's importance is given full value, then childcare will also assume great importance. Modern studies of child development reveal what a complex, delicate process growing up can be. The more we know, the more we realize the supreme need for love and wisdom in childcare. Even if infancy and early childhood are not as crucial as some psychologists maintain, they are extremely important. The adult-centered past all but ignored the child's development before puberty, illustrating this attitude by dressing the child as a miniature man. The history of changing viewpoints toward children is a study of its own, but by now few could deny that parents have a tremendous responsibility in the formation of their children. The mother who carries the child and nurses it is particularly important in the early stages of its development. But the attitudes and atmosphere engendered by both parents—their love for each other, their love and acceptance of the child—can benefit or warp the whole personality. Added to this tremendous responsibility is the fact that the human person whom God has given into its parents' care will exist not only on this earth but for all eternity. If each individual child is of such importance, created by God for an eternal destiny, then there is no more responsible vocation than parenthood.

The traditional Christian approach to family life has preserved the great truth of the dignity of procreation and education of children. It is the privilege and blessing of marriage to cooperate with God in the creation of new human beings. As nothing is more important than the human person, so the family devoted to the loving care of individuals is as valuable as the larger society. The family has always been enjoined to be a model of Christian love and unity. Parents, in particular, are responsible for their children's development within an atmosphere of charity. They are, in the traditional phrase, to provide "a paradise" upon earth for their children; love can make parental sacrifices a joy.

The Christian principle, then, is that persons, each beginning as a child, are precious simply for Christ's sake. God has given man the miraculous power to reproduce his kind, and each new child is a unique and wonder-full addition to the creation. Furthermore, the law of our creation in love is abundance, so much so that there exists a lavish proliferation of everything from stars to animal species. Man is to "increase and multiply" . . . "to be fruitful," and to fulfill the promise to Abraham: "your descendants shall be as numerous as the stars in the heavens." Christ said that each woman would forget anguish "at her joy that a man had come into the world." Love and joy generously rejoice at each new addition to the creation; there is in Christianity an abstract valuation of the process of procreation. It is the fashion these days to make scornful references to "fertility cults," "house-cramming broods," or to women as "baby-machines." Such phrases miss the fact that each birth "statistic" is a person, a miraculous creation of a loving God destined for eternal life. Such language bespeaks the essential attitude—only those grossly indifferent to man's spiritual nature could speak of men and women as "breeding."

This is not to say, however, that the abstract value of abundance is not subject to limitations in concrete situations. Alas, in our world limited by time, space and material resources, the command "to increase and multiply" can conflict with man's other mission to "subdue the world." Indeed, "for the sake of the Kingdom" Christian virginity can renounce all procreation. If in the case of the married the creation of more people would seriously harm the life of existing people, then birth limitation can become a Christian responsibility. More specifically, the care of persons in a particular family or in a particular society can be endangered by additional children. Ironically, this new population problem of the world has been caused by mortality control. Easily administered medical discoveries (vaccination, drugs, insecticides) have saved countless lives—and created imbalances in populations. The lesson seems clear: if God has given man's reason the power to save millions from early death, then He also expects man's reason to provide a good life for them. If the utilization of every resource is not enough, or practically impossible, birth limitation for the good of those already living is rational and good.

Moreover, in the changed conditions of urban life, providing "a good life" is not a simple process. Every child can now be nourished, immunized, and their physical defects corrected (teeth, eyes, feet) to a degree unknown and impossible in former times. In the past, children fell sick, stayed defective, and even died without a parental sense of guilt; who could do anything else anyway? Parents perhaps suffered more, but felt less guilty. Childcare in general may have been less arduous, and with less need of constant supervision to protect children from cars, strangers, electricity, detergents, medicines and machines. Certainly, intellectual and psychological requirements were simpler. Children did not need to be supported through sixteen to eighteen years of schooling to take a respected place in society. Nor, in a less mobile, changing society, did they need as much training in behavior or as much emtional reassurance. Even religious training did not have to compete with conflicting values in such acute forms. The stable community could enforce norms of behavior. Our free, fluid industrialized society requires more carefully prepared people in every sphere. And, except in extreme cases of poverty, there is little help from our society (or from the child himself) in carrying the economic and social burdens of family life. Parents alone are responsible for an enormous economic and psychological effort with each additional child they bear. Under such conditions, the number of children each family can handle becomes crucial.

Providentially, this time of crisis in society and the family has been met by increased medical knowledge of human re-

production. The recent discoveries of the ovulation process
have opened new vistas in the control of fertility. Developments in this field are at present in a state of flux, medically
and morally, but this much is sure: new knowledge brings
new responsibility. Soon, very soon perhaps, a certain means
of limiting fertility will be available. Even now at this stage
of development, when Catholics know of the fertile period
during the monthly cycle, they are responsible for their actions during that time. Choice is unavoidable, for to ignore
knowledge is in reality to choose. Knowledge brings power
over the creative process, but with this new freedom there are
new areas of judgment. God will hold us responsible for
those things which we can morally control. Now that heroic
abstinence is not the only acceptable method of birth limitation, more Catholic parents are responsible for the size of
their families.

Fortunately, the Church has recognized these changes and
gradually has been developing its teaching upon marriage.
The excessively supernatural approach has given way to real-
istic appraisals of the need for family planning. As one example of this, consider how the "serious reasons" needed for
a couple's use of rhythm have been given an ever widened
interpretation. The so-called "indications" for using rhythm
have been extended from strictly biological factors of health
to include social and psychological problems. A country's
over-population is a serious reason. Within a family, fatigue,
strain, tension, and turmoil are recognized as the enemies of
Christian joy, peace, order and abundance. New births with
new pressures can be justifiably avoided. More and more
writers upon Christian family life stress the need for spacing
and limiting children in order to meet more subtle non-
material needs. Certainly, a margin of family leisure and ma-

terial abundance is essential for developing cultural and intellectual values. Deprivation of one's existing children is not an acceptable Christian sacrifice.

At this point, a word is in order describing the enthusiastic movement to sanctify family life that arose in American Catholic circles a little before the Second World War and flowered in the forties. Devout Catholic couples seeking perfection earnestly tried to sanctify family life. But in the attempts to make every aspect of life holy, certain rigid assumptions were made. Perfect Christian families were to be big, unplanned (children coming whenever God sent them), very poor, and if possible live on the land. Liturgical family devotions would abound, and family life would approximate as nearly as possible the peace, harmony and worship of a Benedictine abbey. The ideal father would be a farmer and the ideal mother would find her vocation in contemplative housework and in the loving care and instruction of her children. The more the family was self-sufficient and less dependent upon the crass materialistic world, the better: it was good to bake your bread and sew your clothes, but better to grow and grind the flour and spin and weave the cloth. The family was to be the center of all life, a self-sufficient cell of the Mystical Body of Christ creating and nourishing new members. The evangelical counsels of perfection were to be lived literally by the married laity who "would be not solicitous" and cast themselves upon Providence.

This was a noble ideal in many ways. These people were seeking to restore something sorely missing from modern life with its frantic business and fevered egoistic search for material success. But the ideal was mistaken on several counts. First of all, the greatest sacrifice, or whatever is hardest, is not always the most Christian course of action. The heroic sacrifices of parents are wrong if made at the cost of their children's development. Secondly, the urban, industrialized world can neither be ignored nor totally rejected. The machine, the city, the modern techniques of life had better be sanctified from within than castigated from afar. Christians cannot "restore all things in Christ" by denial. Or rather, every Christian and every Christian family can not. Indeed, the third mistake of this group was to assume that marriage was an automatic, autonomous vocation. The husband's responsibility was simply to support the large family and every wife was confined to childbearing and homemaking for the children "God sent."

But things are not that simple. Not only does God not send children by Himself, but individual Christians may have many talents and many responsibilities to the world. All Christians cannot make all their contributions through identical family patterns. Marriage and childrearing can be the condition within which one functions rather than a full-scale, full-time vocation in the world. The large family requiring all the energy and effort of both parents is not right for everyone.

This truth has been recognized by all in the case of the husband. The father has been granted a responsibility to the world and his own talents; he is now "the emerging layman." Everyone now deplores the fact, for instance, that there have been all too many cases where good and dedicated teachers have been forced to leave teaching in order to support an ever-growing family. The conflict between family life and professional life can become very real. Most moralists viewing such a situation would agree. While abstractly nothing is more precious and valuable than another child, concretely, a family in which another child would mean the sacrifice of the father's vocation in the world would be better off with fewer members. A father trapped in an unrewarding or frustrating job beneath his capabilities is bad for the family and society as a whole. He has a duty to develop his potential contribution outside the family as well as safeguard his family's support and welfare.

But what about the mother? Here is the crux of Christian conscience today. Family planning is admitted for the good of the society, the good of one's children, right also for safeguarding the father's vocation, but can a woman plan her family in order to pursue other work in the world beyond her family? Can she too have a vocation within a vocation? My whole argument in this book so far has been just this: that the Christian freedom of women is not limited because of their sex. The feminine sex has no ready-made vocation. Married women, like married men, have a primary responsibility to their family, but need not find a complete vocation or full use of their talents in childrearing. The traditional role of mother, homemaker, and guardian of culture is a satisfying and wonderful one, but it cannot be imposed upon every married woman. Christian marriage implies procreation and education of children, but it does not of itself demand large numbers of children, or imply that women must limit themselves exclusively to childrearing or homemaking.

While I would maintain the ideal that every man and woman marrying be from the beginning open to the child's arrival, the arrival of more children, and how many more, should be determined by the vocations within a vocation of the parents, especially of the mother. If a Christian couple can use acceptable means of fertility regulation for the fulfillment of the children, for the fulfillment of the father, they can also use it for the fulfillment of the mother. Family planning is for the whole family's welfare, as well as for the larger human family, the Church and the world. Marriage and childrearing does not relieve men and women of responsibility for their own talents or for the needs of the community. In our world and in our time married Christian women can justifiably limit or space their families in order to run for office, practice medicine, nurse, teach, or follow any other good calling whether supposedly feminine or not.

But making these complex decisions is not easy; it is no wonder women are confused. Each individual married woman will have a different situation to judge. The basic principle which will apply to all is that of self-knowledge and love of others. Love of others will rule out decisions that would harm husband or existing children, but beyond this basic minimum, what? Here self-knowledge is necessary and perhaps best obtained by a ruthless self-appraisal. Answering searching questions honestly will help. What capabilities and talents do I have? Are they being used in my present situation? If not, why not? What levels of energy do I possess, and more important, what kinds of energy do I have? The kinds of energy differ in different people: what will exhaust one woman will exhilarate another. The goal is to have one's physical, social, and intellectual energies properly stimulated and challenged in the proper proportions. Again, which role, or mixture of roles, can I most creatively live? Am I, in fact, as good, or as poor a mother, as I think I am?

A subjective consideration is also important here. What am I most happy doing? Catholics have been so fearful of hedonism that happiness has become suspect. But the truth is that God leads us by our human inclinations, *if* we are moving towards Him and genuinely seeking His will. A certain amount of time (and pain) is needed to grow into any vocation, but if one is perpetually desperate and unhappy, then one should try to modify the situation. If, for instance, housework and childcare drive a woman frantic, then following an abstract ideal of a large family is probably not God's will for *her*. If, on the other hand, a woman's small family and outside activity or employment result in a frazzled yet empty existence, then in our affluent part of the world a large family and fulltime homemaking may be right for her. For those who live in countries facing a population problem, or who cannot medically or financially afford more children of their own, there are thousands of institutionalized children in desperate need of love and care. Certainly nothing could be greater work than to rear a cast-off child.

The key to making these vocational decisions is a prudent weighing of abstract values and goods in the light of one's personal, concrete existence. Prayer and the sacraments will of course be a vital means of finding God's will. In the end, only prayer can enable one to "pray beyond preference" while being guided by preference. The thing *not* to be guided by is a prevailing mystique or counter-mystique, for there are many different and equally Christian patterns of marriage and family life. God has made each person different and does not expect all to serve in the same way. In the religious life, everyone does not have to be a Trappist monk; and every married woman is not a ready-made contemplative finding fulfillment in manual labor and childcare. But those who are should seek the traditional feminine role within the home. Other women just as validly should seek to work mainly outside the home, and still others, perhaps the majority, will seek a middle way, half-in, half-out of the home. Each could claim to be exercising their Christian freedom, though living in very different ways.

Yet there is still one pitfall to be avoided, that is, the ever-present danger of self-deceit. Right now, in our culture, especially among the upper-middle classes, the sacrifices of childrearing are greater than the sacrifices required to work in the world. The traditional role is downgraded in our

achievement-oriented society (achievement being the respectable incarnation of success, or Mammon). If women decide
that their vocation is outside the home, it must not be merely
to gain status, and get their share of fame and fortune. Self-
fulfillment and selfishness are not the same, but the latter can
be disguised as the former all too easily—and always under
the guise of freedom. When a family's "contraceptive mentality" is deplored, the target is not so much birth limitation
as the selfish reasons and emotions motivating birth control.

Now that Catholics can also plan families, they must take
care to continue to emphasize the virtues of generosity and
self-giving love. They must re-emphasize the values of children and childcare while at the same time defending new
horizons and freedoms for women. Children remain the
privilege and blessing of married life, and this privilege
should be denied only because of other positive commitments, not through negative selfishness. One can also be selfish in an inordinate desire to create children, but since
children require so much effort many avoid the responsibility for new life for all the wrong reasons. Above all,
increased rational control must be accompanied by a willing-
ness to accept "accidents." Once conceived, the potential
child's right to life and love must be sacred and inviolate. If
a dreadful tolerance of abortion is to be avoided, Christians
must take the initiative in creating a climate of positive planning in which one plans but remains open to a change of
those plans. A certain detachment and flexibility are absolutely necessary for all human planners exercising rational
control (over anything, really); for the tendency is to become
so enamoured with one's own plan that anything or anybody
who gets in the way must go. The human will enthrones
itself with such ease that all power requires humility and
restraint to avoid destructiveness. Rational control must be

integrated within the context of a humble love of God's will and God's creation. Men and women have a wondrous new power over procreation, and they must use it well.

Once the freedom to plan a family has been recognized, the next question concerns the rearing of children. If there is a Christian freedom to plan families, is there also a Christian freedom to determine the kind of childcare and education one's children will get? Does the Christian commitment to love, care and educate the child admit, indiscriminately, to any pattern of childcare? This point is certainly crucial in discussion of married women choosing non-traditional vocations. Even in the small family with the mother committed to a vocation outside the home, many years of intensive childcare are necessary. Who will give this care? Does it make any difference if the mother does not? Can the traditional division of labor between the sexes in the traditional family be changed without harming the children?

First comes the question of whether the children need care (and different care) from both sexes. Many critics of present-day American culture have been concerned by the overwhelming presence of women and the absence of men in the early life of the young child at home and school. There is a real point in this concern. Children of both sexes need care from adults of both sexes: mothers, fathers, and male and female teachers. If the whole process of identification with one's sexual nature proceeds as some psychologists now think it does, it is crucial that each child have appropriate models of his or her own sex. A beloved mother or father, and their substitutes, can make the child happy with the knowledge that he or she is physically like the admired person and will grow up to be even more so. Physical sexual identity can then be accepted happily and integrated within the whole of life.

A beloved parent of the opposite sex also prepares the child for adult love and marriage by helping him or her to respond positively to all persons of the opposite sex.

But do the men and women raising children have to exemplify distinct and opposite sexual roles and characteristics? Is there more than physical identity involved? Some observers bemoan, for instance, not the father's absence, but his lack of "masculinity" and dominance. In their eyes, all is lost if mothers are not accepting, loving and nurturing, and fathers aggressive, dominating and demanding. If there is no great difference in sex roles, this argument goes, then children will grow up confused and disturbed. But behind this reasoning is the prior assumption that the traditional patterns of behavior are innate or so engrained as to be unchangeable. It is just as feasible, however, to maintain that sex roles beyond reproduction are learned and not the sole result of hormones; then one can justifiably advocate that the culture be changed, beginning the process of relearning in the home. We have already said that Christian maturity entails that both sexes exemplify both the traditional masculine and feminine attributes. Moreover, physical integrity can be maintained and reproductive differences delighted in, without personalities and work roles in society being conditioned along sexual divisions. It is the attractive physical presence of both sexes that is necessary to the child, not the example of personality differences and role differences in men and women. The men and women that the child loves should be complete human beings, both warm and loving, and demanding and competent, depending upon the demands of the situation. Beyond reproduction the roles of men and women need not be highly differentiated. If a mother accepts pregnancies and nursing with joy, and a father delights in paternity, it is enough.

Even if initially there were mild confusions over work roles, it would be less costly to the individual than the present system of typing certain characteristics "masculine" or "feminine." When any rigid, long-established pattern first gives way, the new freedom can result in initial bewilderment, yet if it is a good development, in the long run it will be more rewarding to individuals and to society. It is good for a child to see his parents and other men and women both loving and competent in many roles, deciding and dividing up work and activities according to individual qualifications. If boys thrive in a patriarchal context, but girls in a matriarchal, why not strive for the good of both sexes in the best of both worlds? Children could then feel free to express and develop all of the potential within them. Nothing would be suppressed because "boys don't do that," or "that's unladylike." Each child would be encouraged to grow up warm, considerate and nurturing, and also full of initiative, daring, and courage. Most vocations would not be sex-determined (automation having taken away the need for men's greater strength) and both boys and girls could prepare themselves for a wider range of activities. Why should science be masculine and ballet feminine? Individuals, uninfluenced by rigid expectations, would be free to do anything.

This furtherance of freedom for the individual would also serve to develop better attitudes between the sexes and an easier identification with one's own sex. There would be little foundation for resentment or envy of the other sex if little were denied a person solely because of femaleness or maleness. Penis envy (if it exists) and womb envy (if it exists) would fade if males were not cut off from childcare and maternal functions and females were not excluded from opportunities and work in the world. How much easier to accept one's body if doing so entails no limiting of personality or

activity! Perhaps the high rate of homosexuality in this country reflects an increase in masculine sensitivity and feminine
initiative without an increase in the freedom and flexibility
of accepted sexual roles. In particular, those male homo-
sexuals who had harsh, brutal fathers (supermasculine) and
smothering mothers (superfeminine) would have benefited
from parents conditioned to a more complete human ideal.
But even aside from this special problem, the child can iden-
tify with his or her own sex and include the whole spectrum
of personality attributes and vocations in the identification.
The emphasis upon physical differences shown in different
dress, ornamentation and physical styles would be enough to
guard sexual identity, the dignity of the body, and the importance of reproduction.

Once similar sex roles are granted along with the participation of both sexes in childcare, the next question facing
Christians is whether they are committed to the proposition
that the most influential men and women in a child's development are the parents? What is the Christian response to
the challenge of various forms of communal childcare now
existing in some societies? The reasoning of those who would
(and do) provide communal childcare is clear: it is useless to
talk about women's freedom, development and contribution
to society without providing a means for the mother to leave
the home. Therefore, day nurseries, boarding schools, or
"children's houses" must be provided to take over the care
of the children. A small proportion of professional workers
in a communal, centralized arrangement can free many
mothers for work outside the home. Does not this cooperation of effort serve both freedom and efficiency?

Unfortunately, at present many of the assumptions behind
the different methods of communal childcare are non-
acceptable to Christians. The unacceptable Soviet assump-

tion is that children belong to the State and are only on loan to the individual family; therefore it is the state's duty and right in the first place to educate and form Soviet citizens. If the family is helped, it is in the interest of the state's formation of new citizens and the state's need for women to contribute to the all-important production. Within the ideal of disciplined collective living, there is no theoretical hindrance to establishing state boarding schools which have a right to raise the new citizen from cradle to college; some of these already exist in the U.S.S.R. The family has no real rights in any case, but a Soviet apologist for the system made the rather dubious claim that "If the child is in a boarding school, where he only sees his parents when they are rested and at liberty to pay him attention, [once or twice a year] the family is strengthened."[1] But such a "strengthened" family is still only a means: the full-time work of all citizens in the interest of the state is the important end.

Christians must start the other way round. Man is made in the image of God; the child belongs to God and is on loan to the parents who cooperated with God in his procreation. The parents, who also belong to God, have the primary right and duty to form their children for Him. Parents may be assisted by the community or state in their task, but they can not hand over their rights or responsibility. Similarly, the work and production of the state is ordered for the family, not the family for work. The individual welfare of mother, child and family is primary, not the state's production. Christians must reject this state philosophy from the beginning.

But what of the more subtle challenge of the Israeli Kibbutzim which are voluntary and dedicated to the common good and fulfillment of individuals? The argument here is that the individual mother and child are best served by turn-

ing out toward the community, that individuals are happier
integrated into a communal ideal when the common goal is
freedom and fulfillment for all, and mothers can work.[2] To
make this even more of a perplexing question, let us imagine
a voluntary Christian community organized like an Israeli
kibbutz. Would children's houses and communal childcare
be wrong if the community was a Christian one and Christian teachers and Christian values were the governing ideal?
After all, the early Christians ate together and shared a
strong communal life. Could not Christian parents in a
Christian community be justified in turning over to the community the greater part of childcare and not just the schooling of older children?

Even under such an ideal situation I do not think communal childcare would be the better way. In the first place,
the responsibility for the child is too awesome a one to be
given to anyone else. Even if someone else may educate better, fewer peope can love a child more than its parents who
share in its physical nature and procreation. Although the
parental instinct of love for progeny may be nothing more
than the extension of self-love, it is a factor working in the
child's favor. In normal people, the fact that one's child re-
sembles one's self and one's mate is an advantage in understanding and caring for him. Moreover, the ratio of one set
of parents to one group of children of different ages provides
the most individual care and attention for each individual
child. No communal system can provide a higher ratio of
adults to children than, say, the average of two parents to
five children. But even if more intensive care could be given,
the value of commitment and continuity would be lost. In
the kibbutzim it is considered an advantage that the women
who care for the children work on shifts and are always fresh
and emotionally less involved.[3] However, it is a truism of

raising anything else, from delicate plants to puppies, that the same person familiar with every stage of the growing thing can do the best job. Most jobs well done (in any sphere) are done well through a continuous mastery and dedication to every relevant detail. Only continuous presence in individual homes by individual parents can provide such a high level of childcare. The most advanced institutions for deprived children recognize this truth by decentralizing to provide the same cottage parents for small numbers of children.

As for emotional involvement, any effort to decrease it within childcare is dangerous indeed. Bad parents can make their children neurotic with too much of the wrong kind of emotional involvement, but it is better to be positively neurotic than to be detached and incapable of intense ties. The kibbutzim children are reported to be loosely attached to their parents, with whom they spend but one hour at night. Instead, they form intense ties with their peer group, the children with whom they are raised in the children's house.[4] Defenders of the communal method report that in this way the children know love and support without all the unhealthy ambiguity and possessiveness of parental love. But cannot attachment to peers be just as "unhealthy," and detrimental to development? Under this system can the individual develop the strength to stand against the values of his peers, or even to question them? The maturing individual who must fight clear of dependence upon his parents can develop an individual autonomy able to judge both parents and peers. Ideally, the tension between a strong family tie and a strong communal influence can be creative, and can better the individual and society.

Also relevant is the fact that variety and traditional values are conserved by individual parents influencing individual

children. The resources of a family can include past wisdom
and perspectives perhaps not included in what current educators think important. Even in our hypothetical Christian
commune, there would always be a danger of stagnation or
even corruption in the values governing childcare. The necessity of continual choice, reappraisals, or even rebellion
can be a creative necessity. Such freedom (and accompany-
ing anxiety) has always characterized the West with its strong
emphasis upon both family ties and society. With all of its
drawbacks, a system that pressures the individual with freedom is preferable to the security of societies with less choice.

Again, it must be stated that the crucial thing to remember in discussing a method of childcare is that it is an integrated part of a total culture and society and can not be
plucked out and enforced in a totally different context. If
you want communal childraising, you must be willing to live
in the communal society that results. Few of the present-day
advocates of the Russian system of childcare would really be
happy within the Russian adult society that is the end result
—and the same goes for kibbutzim, primitive communal societies, or cultures with extended family systems. In none of
these can any individual oppose "the system" with impunity.
If you want, or if you have to cope with a changing, mobile,
relativistic, open, and above all confusing free society, you
must provide an individualistic method of childcare that
fosters inner security and internalized values by intense
individual nurturing.

But then, goes the familiar argument, no one is proposing
"children's houses" in the West. What our free societies need
are many, many more daycare centers where children of
working mothers can be given professional care, either all
day or after school, and also more public nursery schools,
and community daycamps for the vacation months. Such

measures would allow women to participate fully in the world of work without harming the children. But would they? Most of the objections to full-scale communal child-care also hold for the daycare center proposals. Unless the home is unusually deprived and disorganized, the individual child can still get more individual care and attention (and love) at home than in any daycare center. Individual freedom, culture styles and internalized moral values can better be taught at home with its distinct familiar environment. More important, home is a backstage, recuperative, relaxing place where the prevailing over-organization of urban industrial life need not exert pressure on the individual. If anything, children in modern culture are already away from home too much; they already compete within too many organized groups, too soon. We may need more communal childcare services, but they should only be supplementary to the home, limited to short periods of time, never an all-day substitute. Our utopia in the West should be based upon individual parental childcare in individual spatial units, that is, at home.

Instead of creating communes, let us create a better solution for woman's freedom and fulfillment. My alternative utopian society is one in which fathers can spend more time at home and take a larger share in childraising while mother shares in work outside the home. This goal does away with the need of communal non-parental childcare. If parents are able to alternate their work in the home, and work outside the home, the children need never be without individual parental love and supervision. How much better that both parents can contribute creatively to the community outside the home as well as take a full share in forming their children. Father and mother can become competent to both raise the children and work outside the home, so that the home and the children's care become a joint enterprise in which each can take responsibility and give nearly equal amounts of time. Alternation is a better principle for the household's division of labor, than qualification by sex. When one parent is at home he or she is the homemaker, and the parent who is out in the world is the efficient worker—for both parents in Utopia have learned to move easily from one role to the other. After childbirth and the earliest months of nursing are over, the child can benefit from his father's care—if the father has developed the traditionally feminine virtues so apparent in the complete humanity of Christ. Similarly, the mother, having developed her full potential, can bring much to the community and the world. The children benefit from parents who both care for them and bring stimulation from the larger community.

There are a few couples who already live this complete life. Flexibility of personality and flexible work schedules are the essential factors in its success. Those few parents with special talents can often work at home and determine their own contacts with employers; under such ideal conditions it is possible to arrange schedules for alternating work and family care. Some couples in teaching can also arrange classes and conferences so that both parents alternate work at home and at school. Then there are the workers who do not work from nine to five, but can arrange shifts throughout the day . . . hospital workers, policemen, etc. For many of these lesser paid groups economic necessity has created alternating roles for husband and wife that some middle-class women might envy. But ideally, economics would not be the determining factor. The change in our traditional customs should arise from the desire of the husband to share more in the work within the family and the desire of the wife to share in the community beyond the home. In this way each could become more completely human, enjoying more unity within the family and greater variety outside it. With the increasing trend toward shorter work days and work weeks there would still remain enough leisure time for the family as a whole to be together.

The most important social measures to press for in the effort to facilitate change would be greater flexibility of work schedules, and more family-centered benefits. Family allowances, medical care and maternity leaves for women are already standard in many free societies. A really revolutionary measure would be family leave for fathers of young families. As fathers become more involved and responsible for the family life, there should be a recognition that family crises of childcare (like new babies) may necessitate the presence of the father at home, for a short time. Family allowances of money are good, but family allowances of time away from work for the father and mother would be even more beneficial. Present systems for the flexible accumulation of leave could be slightly expanded for men and women so that the myriad variables in family schedules could be met with a parent's presence. This would be far better than other proposed measures such as home visitor services. The idea of leaving a small sick child with a stranger—albeit a visiting nurse—is repellent. It is just the emergency situations that most require parents.

At the opposite extreme, the triumphs and high points of the child's life in the world also require parental presence. The practice of giving "time off" for school events is very sound, and hopefully will flourish. If both parents are on call and allowed flexibility in work schedules, then the ups and downs of family life could be met without slighting either children or work. With changes in our work patterns and family benefits, women could enter fields that require high dedication and continuity of effort without harming the children. If the family were equally the father's responsibility and he too was given flexibility in schedules, then a crisis could be met by the parent who was not at a critical moment in his or her work outside the home. With his wife sharing the economic burdens a father could "afford" more time for the family. Perhaps our murderous lower-class moonlighting and middle-class prestige-race could be modified by diffusion: let men and women share in each other's satisfactions and pressures. We might at least be able to even out the death rate, so that women would not bury their husbands with such regularity. In the final analysis, perhaps fathers need home, children and "feminine" values far more than mothers need more participation in the world.

But while waiting for society's change and helping bring it about, what can the mother do who does not choose the traditional role? She cannot depend upon family allowances, maternity benefits, family leave, homemaker services, public nursery schools, camps or flexible part-time work or schooling. Her husband probably cannot "get off" or afford to give much time to the family, even if he were prepared to do so. There is one more solution for women widely recommended —that is, the mother-substitute in the home. The mother-substitute comes into the home and takes over so that the mother can go out to work outside the home. Such an arrangement keeps the values of individual care and a home-centered culture. The parents who provide the substitute still set the standards for childcare. Continuity can be achieved and the security of home and household routine is uninterrupted. If a mother-substitute can be found so that a warm loving mother can spend time away from home, can there be any possible objections?

Again, unfortunately, there are theoretical reservations as

well as enormous practical difficulties. There is with substitute mothering the lessening of the emotional ties with the parents as well as the seriousness of handing over the responsibility of childcare to someone else. In addition to the danger of depriving or confusing the development of the child, there is the serious deprivation of the parents within such a system. With a full-time nurse the joys, delights and the challenge of childcare can be denied parents, almost as completely as in the communal systems of childcare. Erik Erikson expresses the importance of parental development with their children in these witty words: "Babies control and bring up their families as much as they are controlled by them; in fact we may say that the family brings up a baby by being brought up by him."[5] Parents and children "growing up together" need each other; a mother substitute who takes over most of the childcare deprives the parents of life's greatest joy and challenge.

But deprived parents could have other compensations, such as more freedom for challenging work, so the crucial question remains whether the child is harmed by parental substitutes in the home. It would seem that parents could delegate the physical care of their children satisfactorily; after all, food, sleep, clothing, baths and medical attention can be measured and checked and easily supervised. Only in an emergency illness or accident would the presence and judgment of the parent be required. But what is really at stake is the psychic development of the child. This is a subtle, complex process in which unconscious attitudes and value judgments are conveyed to the child. Just how this happens is not altogether clear. Many believe that the important intangibles are conveyed throughout the physical routine of feeding, changing, and play. Emotional tones, the amount of stimulation and response given to the child's physical and intellectual reactions—all of these unmeasurable things may shape a child's personality. Certainly, the child's conscious attitude to love, religion, sex, danger, death, race, and culture of the world will be shaped by the instruction of the person who cares for him. The inter-personal relationships children experience are crucial; it is hazardous to delegate this responsibility.

The fact that it has been delegated in other cultures has little bearing on twentieth-century life. Successful substitute mothering, like communal childraising, works only when all women in a culture are homogeneous and/or there is a rigid code of behavior to which all members of the society will conform. The dreadful English system of strict nannies and early boarding school imposed much suffering on the children of the upper classes, but they were able to survive and function within a formal adult society with strict class lines and group conformity to unchanging standards of behavior. Now that the Empire, stately homes and class certainties have all become obsolete, even the English are forced into reappraisals. Like other changing societies, they are facing the situation of America, which has always been mobile. Modern life does not stand still long enough to possess the stability in which loving servants can be incorporated into an individual family's life and values. Most intermediaries between children and parents cannot be trusted to share the parents' outlook or values. Economic discrepancies in status mean wide discrepancies in culture. Since all levels concur in their avoidance of domestic service, few women will consider becoming full-time servants. Unfortunately, the available women will most often be those who are too punitive or too permissive with children, quite apart from their inability to stimulate the child intellectually.

But before going on with the practical difficulties of find-

ing a satisfactory mother substitute, I would like to discuss
the inadequacies of the clichés that crop up in the discussion
of women leaving home. Repeatedly, it is stated that "it is
not the quantity of time spent with the child, but the quality"; or (just as confidently) "better to have a happy mother
for a short time than an unhappy frustrated mother all day."
I can't help but wonder about these standby justifications
and the assumptions behind them. Can a small child distinguish quality of time from quantity of time, or, in a child's
world, does not quantity of time merge with quality? Certainly, the pre-rational child cannot understand about outside commitments to good causes. Absence, in the child's
primitive, unsubtle world, means going away, a basic form of
rejection. To the primitive, only concrete care and presence
prove love. When all communication is physical and emotional, mother is who mothering does. Since the very small
child lives only in the present, it is doubtful whether he can
be influenced or much nurtured in a very small part of his
waking day. A marvelous hour in the evening does not help
a small child during the long hours of his day, for he lives
only in the now. Before speech it is sensory and physical
contact which counts; flesh speaketh to flesh.

But will not unhappy mothers convey through this very
"flesh" their unhappiness and resentments if they are forced
to take care of their children instead of working outside the
home? I wonder. A few mothers may really be so inadequate
and hostile that anyone else would do better; but the majority of normal women (who are mature enough, after all,
to work successfully) can also do a good job with their children—even if frustrated. Only the grossly immature will
"take out" frustrations upon their children; and who knows,
perhaps even these children would still choose to have their
own frustrated mothers rather than someone else. And I

might add that the someone else in these arguments is usually presented as a competent, warm, motherly woman delighted to be a mother substitute. The assumption is that
this perfect Mrs. Santa Claus will never get bored or frustrated or unhappy for she, somehow, will be impervious to
the developments and influences which make educated mothers unhappy. In other words, it is a stoutly maintained
maxim that "the good hireling" is as good, if not better, for
the lambs.

The reasoning of this approach is shaky indeed. Too much
is granted to the "feeling" of the mother in question; if she
feels right about leaving her children, then it is right. The
argument holds that some women may work full-time a week
after the baby is born, some only after the child goes to
school, but if mother thinks she is making the right decision,
then it *is* the right decision for her. And what about the
child? Will a mother's easy conscience really solve all problems? Certainly not. Mothers in primitive tribes have con-
scientiously denied their children vital modern medicine;
mothers in our society have beaten and starved their children without a qualm. The subjective criterion of a mother
"feeling right about it" is ridiculous. Even the children's
feelings are not a good guide, since a deprived child may
know nothing else. Instead of relying solely on personal emotions, an objective standard of proper care and emotional
and psychic stimulation should be sought. The variables in
the situation will instead be the age of the child, the quality
of the person caring for one's children, and the quantity of
time a substitute substitutes. When, however, the search for
the qualified mother-substitute begins, so do the practical
difficulties.

Perhaps the most trying problem is the previous generation's ideas about childraising. The older women who are

available (and are not trained for other kinds of more highly paid work) often suffer from sexual taboos and standards of cleanliness that can be harmful to small children. Most educated young mothers will clash with older women who often think that children should be on rigid feeding schedules, or trained at eight months, or not allowed to get dirty. The creative outlets recommended for children today, water-play, modeling clay, paints, blocks, etc., effectively destroy the traditional standards of housekeeping of women who do domestic work. Older mother-substitutes rarely encourage or tolerate disorderly creativity or allow the child enough freedom to roam and experiment. Conscientious baby-sitters will fearfully choose the safe and tidy way; lots of television and little interaction with the neighborhood children.

At the opposite extreme, a young girl, or even some older baby-sitters who can see things from the child's viewpoint, may indeed be childlike and lack responsibility. Then children get out of hand from too little discipline and supervision. Nor do these warm, permissive primitives know how to stimulate the child's intellect by reading, conversation or creative play. Back to T.V. again as the easy way out. But as all children do not function well in unstimulated, bored states, mother-substitutes like some mothers create behavior problems. If there are several children in the family, then partiality to the good children and preferential comparisons from babysitters can be as dangerous as from parents. Women who care for the children over a long period of time can also get emotionally involved in an unhealthy way. In short, it is almost as hard to find a satisfactory full-time mother-substitute as it is to be a good mother.

The hard fact that must be recognized, as many a mother realizes, is that if a person were as well-equipped as herself, she would not be available. Young, energetic, creative, educated, cultured women do not hire out for childcare. If they did, and one appeared who would love and stimulate all one's children, she would be too high in status to also cook and clean. Several servants would be needed to replace many a young mother who combines knowledge and skill in child-care with household management. Educated women may feel frustrated in many ways, but most of them stay home while their children are young because they honestly recognize that no one available can do a better job. Unfortunately, many young children *will* suffer if their mothers work full-time; many working mothers *should* feel guilty. How many of "the wonderful women" working mothers have taking their place are really all that "wonderful" from an objective point of view? Women must be as alert to selfish self-deceit in judging their decision to leave home as they are in judging their irresponsible waste of useful talents.

When it becomes a case of mother or children, and it can, Christian women, who are instructed "to lay down their lives" for their brethren, should certainly be willing to sac-rifice fulfillment outside of the home. Reality and mature love may present inescapable crosses which cannot be ration-alized or organized out of existence. There may be children who cannot adjust to substitute care, and there are places where no good care is available. If despite one's best efforts some child begins to show harmful effects from lack of proper mothering, the Christian mother, or father, must be prepared to sacrifice his or her own fulfillment to respond to the child's need. The mother's professional status cannot be an independent higher value over and against the family.

The new-style feminists urging women into professions regularly take an opposite view. One author describing the professional mother's qualifications says: "She can be wor-ried about her children, but the show must go on . . . she and her children have to learn somehow—and very early—to accept her professional status."[6] The Christian (and many others) will answer just as emphatically "but what *show* could be more important?" Another disturbing example of this diffidence occurs in Betty Friedan's book when she relates the sad case of a Catholic woman who stops outside political activity because, beside the disapproval of priest and husband, the school psychologist claimed that her child's school work was being harmed.[7] Mrs. Friedan's only concern was that this woman (as typical of many backward orthodox types) was being frustrated. There was absolutely no discussion of whether the child was, or was not, being harmed by her mother's absence. If she was, what then? The difficult ethic of sacrificial love would say: this mother was right to come home, and defer her own fulfillment. The time that we have our children is short; if we fail at a crucial point in their development, the effects may last their lifetime. Facile assumptions that no children are ever harmed by absent mothers do not convince conscientious women who may have experience to the contrary.

Nor can Christian women be satisfied with a mere "no harm done" standard. If working outside the home will mean that one's children are not given "the extras" of family life, that too will make women hesitate. The standards of love cannot be minimal; Christians are committed to fullness, abundance, happiness—all the more than necessary things that can create a "paradise," or "happy enclave in this vale of tears." The traditional language may be overly sentimental, but the concept is valid: the Christian family cannot just survive at a tolerable level. We now realize that it is a Christian responsibility to limit families so that the existing children may have an abundant life; but it will be self-defeating if we limit the number of children and also countenance less loving attention to the children by their parents. How ironic if children of small affluent families with working mothers get less nurturing in the end than the child from the struggling overcrowded family. A child can be just as rejected when he disrupts a mother's outside fulfillment as when he strains the emotional and material resources of a big family. The dark side of women's semi-emancipation from the home is the subtle pressures upon children to grow up in a hurry so that mother can get out. Every nursery school has children who have been sent there too early so that the mother can leave home.

So where are we? Have I really spent a whole book justifying woman's freedom from the traditional role, only in the end to say, "yes, but until society changes, you must sacrifice yourself and stay home for your children"? My disapproval of communal childraising and emphasis upon the drawbacks of mother-substitutes may give the impression that things are hopeless. Proposals for the husband's return and flexibility of work schedules in society, are obviously not widely applicable now, nor will they be in the near future. Since we do not have flexible schedules or family benefits, must a woman who feels called to a non-traditional role have one or two children and mark time while they grow up? Fortunately, I think there is more room to maneuver in our present transitional society.

At present, despite drawbacks, the best means of maneuvering work outside the home remains the mother-substitute. There are less serious theoretical and practical difficulties in this solution than in communal childcare. Having already stated the problems, I can now make the distinctions which modify the negative factors. First of all, there is the rare case when a mother can find (and afford) a paragon of all motherly virtues combined with experience and knowledge of modern childcare. Obviously, with the perfect mother-substitute, a mother can leave home for longer periods of time. But even with perfection I think that a guiding rule of substitute parental care in the home should hold.

This principle is that parents can insure their primary influence upon their child by personally caring for him during the major portion of the child's waking day at home. This rough rule of thumb takes account of the difference in the ages of one's children. The school-age child can stay up later at night and spends some six hours away from the home during the day. Even a full-time working mother could spend the greater part of her child's day at home with him. Weekends, vacations, and the independent outside social activities of older children would balance out in time so that the parents rather than a substitute would rear their children. Besides, older children can differentiate time in an adult way, postpone important questions, and benefit from intensive times of mothering. An exceptionally energetic woman, with a cooperative husband, a good mother-substitute, and a smallish school-age family can work full-time away from home and do as good a job as a full-time mother. There may even be advantages to the children from the stimulation mother brings home from the world outside the home.

However, such stimulation is lost upon a child who cannot communicate verbally or measure time. The small pre-school child may not distinguish quality from quantity, and it is extremely important that he have his mother or father for most of his waking day. A mother working away from home on a nine-to-six schedule will not see enough of a child who goes to bed at seven, to be the primary influence upon his development. If it is a case of dire necessity, then the child may not be harmed; since the mother's lack of choice in leaving can probably be sensed. But if there is any freedom of choice, the mother of a small child should make sacrifices in order to spend the greater part of his waking day with him.

The key word here is "waking," for the small child also sleeps during the day. If the mother can schedule part-time work so that her substitute is there while the child sleeps, plus some hours before or after the nap, then she can still be away half the working day and yet with the child most of *his* day. Obviously, work that could be done in the evenings after bedtime would also be a good arrangement as would work on weekends when father would be home. Work on several days a week might also be managed. The irony is that many, many energetic women with pre-school children and a minimum of outside help could still manage a forty-hour work week if they could arrange *which* forty hours they would work. Even if the present working-day schedules were simpy divided into two shifts, many less energetic women could manage twenty hours or so a week without neglecting their pre-school children.

With the basic principle of required parental time and influence, let us outline a life pattern for women attempting to integrate marriage, work and children. Naturally, some of their relevant problems and decisions would pertain to the woman choosing a semi-traditional vocation as well, but the woman committed to serious long-range outside work has the newest and most difficult problems to face. How can she pursue her vocation within a vocation?

First of all a woman should prepare herself for her work in the world as well as for marriage and childrearing. Hopefully, she will not marry until she knows who she is and what she wants to do, and has finished her basic training and education. This preliminary preparation (with its implication of greater maturity) helps a marriage. Not only will the hus-

band know at the beginning that his wife wants to participate in outside work, but if the wife is already thoroughly
established, she can welcome pregnancy without worry over
her incomplete education. It seems much more consistent
with Christian ideals to defer marriage (as long as possible,
anyway) rather than enter a marriage in which a child will
be a calamity. Mature Christian love will desire early frui-
tion in the creation of a child; and every child has the right
to be joyfully accepted as a blessing rather than as a serious
inconvenience. The ideal solution is to marry hoping for an
early pregnancy, but planning upon the continuation of
one's work until shortly before the birth of the child.

  With the birth of her first baby our non-traditional
woman would take leave of absence from outside work, or
schooling. It is extremely important that the mother in her
"novitiate" be free from pressure, feel leisured, and fully re-
cuperate her health. Successful nursing and relaxed handling
of a first child depend upon a rested, calm mother who is not
in a hurry and can spend time simply contemplating the
marvel she has produced. A kind of honeymoon with the
baby is needed, as well as lots of extra time to see that one's
husband is not ignored or left out of this adjustment. Most
women will find that they have all they can successfully
handle with a first baby and a first father without formal outside commitments. But it is also important during this time
that one's outside work not be totally dropped. While making her initial adjustment to childcare, the new mother must
not neglect her other commitment. This might be managed
by research, a reading program, a mastery of a new skill
(such as a language), occasional attendance at important
meetings, or perhaps a small creative project in one's field—
in short, anything that can be done at home while baby
sleeps or scheduled in short sorties away from home. Every

mother should get away from the baby for short periods anyway; if only to avoid anxieties and neurotic over-concentration on her child. The non-traditional mother must simply channel these relief activities towards her other work. She can read professional journals instead of magazines, go to class instead of bridge evenings and to the library instead of teas and luncheons.

When the earliest and most important months of nursing are over, or in some cases an even longer adjustment period has passed, a new possibility may be sought. In a very few cases maternity leaves might enable the mother to return to her old job part-time. But in most circumstances, this next stage can only be managed by finding some unusual opening in one's field, or perhaps by engaging in more study or private preparation. At any rate the effort to continue and renew outside work on a part-time basis is salutary. This part of a woman's vocation is important enough to warrant family planning—in this case for the sake of the mother's long-range fulfillment in her outside work. But this increased commitment can take place if, and only if, a good part-time mother-substitute can be found to give baby an outing, feed him, say, one meal, and perhaps do light housekeeping during his nap. If economics or other circumstances make this impossible, even with sacrifice of the artificially high American standard of new furniture, cars, clothes, and entertainment, this stage of gradual half-in, half-out out of the home can be still more informal. Perhaps an exchange with other neighboring young mothers with babies can be arranged; or at least night or weekend activities while husband babysits.

However, if most couples will put the wife's "career" before new cars, picture-book homes, and other luxuries, there can be enough money to provide for part-time help or schooling which (coldbloodedly) in the long run will benefit the family through increased earning capacity. This "invest-ment" in the wife's training and outside work should con-tinue throughout the childbearing period. Part-time work outside may not be financially profitable, but it keeps the non-traditional wife psychically balanced and able to resume full-time work with ease. Outside contacts keep the mother's full potential active, easing the strains and completing the joy of the childbearing years. Spacing the children in order to allow mother to keep some outside commitments is a valid moral reason for family planning.

After birth, infancy and babyhood come the school years when the child is eager to leave mother for companions and his own world. Nursery school is a first step on this road and a good thing for most children. But a caution must be inter-jected here. Mediocre nursery schools resorted to in despera-tion can really do harm to a small child's development. Since there are no public nursery schools with required standards, there are really very few excellent schools; and where they exist they are extremely expensive. Furthermore, any mother who thinks that a child in nursery school will alone free her for a formal job on a rigid schedule has never experienced the ins and outs of such schools. There are numerous ex-tended vacations and children with so much as a sniffle are sent home so as not to infect the others. However, the in-cubation period of most childhood diseases is undetectable, and the small child can literally spend more time at home sick than at school. Furthermore, all good schools try to in-volve the mothers as co-educator, so that there are school parties and exhibits which a working mother must miss. The child whose mother cannot come feels left out. Unfortu-nately, this is often the same child who is pushed into nur-sery school too soon. If a mother who works cannot afford both help and nursery school, I think the money and effort could be more safely spent on a good helper, and excellent play equipment at home. It is probably better for a working mother to arrange informal play groups when she is home.

However at six or so, children must go to school and are gone for most of the day. They can take a meal at school, and are somewhat hardened to the surrounding germs. When the youngest child goes off to school, a more formal commitment to outside work can be made. If a woman has unusual energy, or more than usual economic resources, she can resume full-time work—with the help of her husband and an excellent substitute homemaker. It is still ideal, however, that a parent rather than a substitute should be home to greet the returning school child. In some ways the subtle supervision of independent older children takes more skill and effort than babycare. Half-time or three-quarters work geared to the school schedule would remain the ideal for most women, especially those who do not have that perfect substitute.

Those women committed to very demanding careers who do return to full-time work would have to be willing to make enormous sacrifices (as would their husbands). They can provide an adequate quantity of time and quality of time with their school-age children only by drastically cutting out their own leisure and recreation activities. With enough self-discipline and asceticism, they can give as much time to career and children as others do to either, but it is hard. It is a question of single-minded drive and individual energy, organizational ability and capacity for sacrifice. The Christian responsibility in each case is to evaluate how well the individuals within the family are doing and determine one's own actions for the common good of all. The rule for decisions during the strenuous years of intensive family responsibilities is again, know yourself, love others, and give enough time to family life.

But the strenuous years do not last forever. In all too short a time children grow up and are ready to leave home for college. At this crisis of separation the woman who has chosen a non-traditional role has an advantage over other mothers, especially those who have not made the effort to continue community contacts. The woman dedicated to outside work can increase her efforts so that she has no sense of uselessness or emptiness. Her income can help pay for her children's schooling and there need be no severe transition from one role to another. In middle-age her absorption in her work and her sense of purpose will make her more impervious to many of the prevalent feminine problems brought on by boredom, fading beauty, and lack of status in a youth-centered culture. Such a committed woman can be an excellent mother to young adults, and the best of all mothers-in-law. She will have experienced the satisfactions and joys of both family and professional life.

This is a happy picture, but life in this world is often unsatisfying and unfair. Many more women than men will by social circumstances be forced to sacrifice many talents for many years. Men and women should both try to change the society for the future; but in the meantime our new woman will have to plan, struggle and connive to carve out a complete and full life and work. If, despite all her efforts, she cannot exercise her freedom, then let her make sacrifice graciously. "Let there be no murmuring," said St. Benedict to his monks, and it is a maxim which could be well taken by more women today. There are already enough shrill, sullen, bitter women among us. It is extremely important that the young mother, who may be forced by the culture and circumstance to bear in isolation a disproportionate burden of childrearing, be especially loving and accepting, for she will be the primary creator of her children's world. How ironic if in pining for work outside the home she fails in the great work at hand. Let her beware the current mystique of work, especially when it becomes a mystique of "the profession." The concept and implications of work need to be examined. Now that women have new freedom, they must ask themselves, what is work, and what are women working for?

NOTES

[1] Quoted by David and Vera Mace, *The Soviet Family* (New York: Doubleday, 1963), p. 288.

[2] Cf. Alice Rossi, "Equality Between the Sexes: an Immodest Proposal," *Daedalus*, Spring, 1964.

[3] Bruno Bettelheim, "Does Communal Education Work? The Case of the Kibbutz," *The Family and the Sexual Revolution*, ed. by Edwin M. Schur (Bloomington: Indiana Univ. Press, 1964), p. 303.

[4] *Ibid.*, p. 304.

[5] Erik Erikson, *Childhood and Society*, 2nd ed. (New York: W. W. Norton, 1963), p. 69.

[6] Ethel J. Alpenfels, "Women in the Professional World," *American Women: The Changing Image*, ed. Beverly B. Cassara (Boston: Beacon Press, 1962), p. 89.

[7] Betty Friedan, *The Feminine Mystique* (New York: W. W. Norton, 1963), p. 352.

SIX

Woman as Worker

A great part of modern woman's confusion today undoubtedly concerns her role as a worker. I have already touched upon problems of working women, and woman's work, but there is no escaping more basic questions about work. What is work essentially? And why is it important to men and women? These deceptively commonplace questions require psychological, philosophical and theological answers. But even beginning answers can help the discussion. It is disturbing when difficult questions are so frequently brushed aside. It is alarming when a counter-mystique of work, especially work-as-a-job, takes the place of the "eternal feminine" solutions.

We are now in what might be called a crisis of work—or perhaps just beginning such a crisis. On the larger stage of society the problems of unemployment, automation and early retirement are forcing reappraisals of the function of work in society and the individual person's life. Perceptive observers of our society have already made the recommendation that the puritan ethic basing income upon employment be changed. When there is no work available for many, then a rich society must seriously consider guaranteed incomes for all regardless of employment. Indeed, a Kenneth Galbraith could envision an affluent society in which only the privileged few could work, "privileged" because, as he recognized, most men desperately want to work.

This desire for work is the more subtle psychological problem. In our society everyone is primarily graded by occupation. People ask not who you are, but "what do you do?" Status is so bound up with work that the rich man who does not work is a rarity. Those who do not work may always eat, but they do not feel worthwhile unless they "earn their keep." After all, from childhood on, a person is constantly questioned, "and what do you want to be when you grow up?" Since the answer is properly this or that occupation, a tremendous personal crisis ensues when a person either cannot get a job, or after identifying himself as a such-and-such for years, suddenly is retired. The anxiety over being worthwhile comes early for the unemployable youngster in a slum, in the middle years for a worker during automation, and late for the professional elite. Age does for the few, what automation and prejudice can do for many. One can even argue that the low status of the aged in our society is not primarily that they are wrinkled and no longer youthful, but that they no longer work. Their real life is over, say the busy workers; and the old, along with the retarded, the mentally ill, and other useless non-workers simply drop from sight.

This utilitarian attitude toward people and productivity colors the modern pragmatic attitude towards intellectual work. By now, anti-intellectualism and its Christian manifestations have been adequately recognized and chronicled. But it is interesting to question whether a concern for useless knowledge and useless people may have some connection. When everything and everybody must prove their worth, in the race against Russia, or the race to the moon, or even ironically, the race for personal creativity, then our healthy respect for results has become a disease of a sick society.

Ironically the heavy pressures to work, produce, to achieve, to fulfill oneself, can make these very goals impossible. The drop-out figures for affluent middle-class students who give up in the midst of college has become a symptom of the basic problem of apathy in the culture as a whole. When all work becomes only a means to achievement, or success, or more bluntly, personal power, then the means to this end become intolerable. One thing at least we are slowly learning about work, it is done best by those who do it mostly for itself alone. Educators, industrial psychologists, and the people in charge of scientists have almost mastered this maxim. Freedom, iniative, and the intrinsic worth of work are championed—all in the interests of greater productivity. Unfortunately worker satisfaction can become simply one more manipulative technique to ensure results.

Another disturbing attitude toward work in modern society is the degraded status of personal service and manual work. Work status is almost in inverse proportion to the amount of physical exertion required. Blue-collar workers must pitch in and keep moving, white-collar workers sit or stand immobilely and use only their hands. Executives may sign their names, make phone calls and travel, but mainly they think and talk. In teaching, nursing, medicine, selling, and myriad other fields it is the same pattern all over again. The less physical exertion, the less direct personal service, the higher one's status. One can almost formulate a law: those who serve should seek to supervise, for money comes from manipulating others from a distance. These values governing our culture become painfully clear when the salary of a teaching teacher is compared to that of a top advertising executive who manipulates the men who manipulate the media for the sake of greater sales to nameless thousands.

Naturally, in such a value structure, domestic work is at

the very bottom of the status-heap. Housekeeping and child-care are so little esteemed that only those at the bottom of the economic ladder even consider it. Every other job is preferred to that of housekeeper and/or nursemaid. The shortage of "help" has become so acute that there are now afoot efforts to upgrade domestic service by training schools and specialization. (A "family dinner specialist" or a "family clothes specialist" would replace cook and laundress.) Laudable as such efforts are, more than this is needed to offset the general disparagement of physical work, and personal service. Obviously, this degraded status is a factor in the unhappiness of many women who are "just housewives." They do not get paid, nor do they get recognition for performing their low-status work. In an age and time when high status is achieved through specialized, mental, abstract work, performed in an organizational and time-measured context, they are working at continuous, unspecialized, physical service tasks either alone or with small children. If they are unhappy they reflect society's estimate, or at least its economic estimate. But is society's low estimate of this work valid? For this answer we again confront conflicting values. The work that is thought worthwhile depends upon the definition of work and its ultimate purpose.

To define work sounds like a relatively simple task until one attempts it. To define work in the limited sense of job or employment is certainly inadequate, for there is work without payment. Whether there can be employment or jobs without work is also a question. What is happening, for instance, when Hollywood stars are paid to attend a premiere movie; is their simple physical presence work? Perhaps so. It could also be maintained that in some minimal sense animals and machines work. But more important, what are the implications of the word "work" used in such phrases as "work of art," "workmanship," "work of God" (*Opus Dei*), or the biblical "work out your salvation in fear and trembling"? Leaving aside philosophical implications, and specifically speaking of man's activity, work can be defined as a conscious attempt to impose order or pattern to meet some internal or external necessity. It is the element of necessity which differentiates work from other activities, such as play, that other important and distinctively human activity.

However, as the external necessity for work recedes and internal necessities increase, all distinctions become more difficult. Work can not really be confined to activity one hates and would avoid if one could. An individual can love his work so much that it is difficult to distinguish it from play. Similarly, the clear-cut canon law distinctions between "servile work" and other kinds of work can also be blurred. If servile work was thought of as manual labor, as against higher intellectual work, this distinction is now unsatisfactory. Such hierarchies of activity and radical separation of physical work and mental work assumed a rigid separation of noble mind from brute body and a static hierarchial habit of thought no longer acceptable to the modern Christian mind. Those religious orders where lay brothers or sisters are relegated to inferior status and limited to servile (i.e., physical) work are gradually changing their ways. Increasingly, each person is recognized as a unified whole who possesses both physical and mental powers and faculties. Obviously certain kinds of work require more mental exertion and others more physical energy, but when a human being works there can never be wholly intellectual or wholly physical labor.

The horror of industrialized assembly lines lies in the attempt to require of man only physical effort. When the same action is repeated over and over, there is no opportunity to exercise the distinctively human capacity for conscious choice and decision in imposing a pattern upon raw material. Man might as well be a machine.[1] For this reason automation should be welcomed, for even with all its attendant problems, at least it will relieve men of work in which a whole area of man's faculties are unused and deadened. Perhaps it will turn out that the fewer attendants of the complex machines at automated factories will have to be more highly trained in more diverse areas of knowledge (say electronics as well as mechanics) and more responsible for a total operation.[2] Man desperately needs this consciousness of the whole pattern he is contributing to by his efforts. The challenge and satisfaction of work arise from ordering various components into a whole. The more diverse, flexible and various these components, the greater the challenge in mastering them and forming something new. Work can, and should be exhilarating as well as tiring; boring repetitive work without intrinsic meaning or challenge is a hundred times more fatiguing than satisfying work. Individuals differ in powers and faculties, but common to all humanity is the inability to stand total boredom; fatigue and an eventual loss of consciousness in sleep are the result. Each organism must have sufficient stimulation to function well, neither too much or too little to do. Inhuman work can bore man into unconsciousness, and complete lack of any work can create not only boredom, but anxiety and suffering as well. Why is work so important and basic to man?

Psychologists define a man's mental health by his ability to love and to work. Work is said to liberate libido; the inner drives which impell man to activity or passivity must be controlled, channeled, and thoroughly mastered when man works. The conscious attempt to apply certain efforts, and just those efforts that are needed, gives man a sense of self, a self which in contact with his environment reacts and shapes it to some purpose. Although the effort may be painful, the order and pattern man succeeds in imposing without, reassures him of his ability to maintain order within himself. When a man can discriminate, suppress, initiate, and develop external things in accordance with his will and decision to create a certain pattern and order, he gains confidence in himself as a person who can freely act or react to external and internal forces. In one sense, a person does create himself, or find himself, through work.

Paradoxically, a person can also "lose himself" in his work. Losing oneself is the other great attraction of work, and perhaps the secret of its necessity for mankind. Work is one way out of the solipsistic bind. Other people and other things must surely exist when I can contact them by working. The satisfaction of work comes partly from the reassurance that the rest of the world exists and I can get to it. When my efforts can make a difference in the environment, then my relationship to that environment is strengthened. The greater absorption required of work, the greater is the relief from the burden of self-consciousness. The worker is self-conscious, but in a released, relaxed, unburdensome way. Anxiety, loneliness and fear can rarely penetrate to the person hard at work. The whole movement toward occupational therapy is based upon this paradox: work helps the person stand alone and at the same time opens the way to the world.

This is not surprising, for Christian theology maintains that God created man to work. Adam and Eve were instructed to increase and multiply and to subdue the earth. In Paradise before the Fall they were to name the animals and to till and dress the garden, an apt symbol of all intellectual and physical work. In this work they were acting as beings made in the image of God. God the Creator is shown in Genesis as a calm Workman creating and ordering the universe. Man as the high point of creation was meant to share in this creativity; his work too was good. Only after the Fall do disorder and discontent attend work. Pain, sweat, thorns, and the ultimate frustration of death will then thwart man in his activity. All of man's efforts will be contradicted if in the end every man and every work will return to dust. Work which in Paradise was a free, God-given, God-like activity, an exercise of man's sovereignty over the world, was after the Fall cursed with necessity and failure. Man's sovereignty over himself and the universe was lost. No matter how great or many his works, symbolized in the tower of Babel reaching toward the sky, he could never fully succeed or restore his lost unity with God and creation.

Only Christ the God-man could restore man and the Creation. Only by participating in Christ's divine life can man's unity within himself and his unity with Creation be restored. In Christ, who came to make all things new, man's work and works will not be contradicted for Christ mastered necessity, pain, thorns, and death. Christ upon the Cross said: "it is finished," and did not "it" refer to His great Work, the salvation of the world? In that great work all of man's work has meaning. The Resurrection removes forever the curse upon work. Pain, frustration, necessity, and death remain, but can not be victorious. While we must still "work out our salvation," Christ's victory has assured the ultimate outcome. In Christ, faith, hope, charity, and good works are possible for man; their possibility wonderfully restores man's humanity. Now a man's life and all of his efforts can have meaning, for men can live and work within the communion of Christ and the Father, Christ and His members, the Church. All things can "work together for good for those who love God." The curse of failure, difficulties, and death can be transformed with new meaning, for a new dimension of life, time and space are assured men. The New Jerusalem must be built and every man's faith and work can contribute.

Not only is all of life now a working out of salvation, but work in its more limited sense is given a new dignity. St. Paul pictures the whole creation groaning for the day of the Lord, waiting for the sanctification and work of men. "All things are yours," he says, but men must express this sovereignty by the perfect fulfillment of everyday work. Wherever you are, whatever you do, you must do it perfectly for the glory of God. There is no good activity or work that does not contribute to God's glory. But there is in Christianity (and in this it is radically opposed to paganism) a prejudice toward manual labor. St. Paul recommends work with the hands, as in his own trade of tentmaking. And more important, Christ Himself spent most of His time on earth working as a carpenter. Most of the apostles labored with their hands, and in the earliest Christian community waited upon tables to serve their brethren. In this direct physical service they were following the explicit example and teaching of Christ. On the most significant of all evenings, as a special sign and lesson, Christ washed the feet of His disciples and revealed this direct physical service as a central expression of Christian life and love. In the new life of the Kingdom the highest will serve most humbly. Moreover, individuals will be judged upon physical acts of service, helping the sick, the imprisoned, the poor, even giving a cup of water in Christ's name. Hearing, believing, preaching (and writing) will be for nought if one does not show forth faith in works.

Unfortunately, while Christians always retained the value of "works of mercy" (as a specialized activity), the importance of everyday work as a part of the whole process of salvation became minimized. Neo-Platonic influences helped create a Christian contempt for this world and a theory of body and spirit that scorned the lower activities of man. Over the centuries, however, each renewal of the Church included again the basic importance of the incarnation and expressed anew a commitment to everyday work. The hermits in the desert worked and judged the spiritual progress of their disciples by their steadfastness in manual labor.[3] The Benedictines dedicated themselves to work and prayer, and significantly, each renewal in their long history has involved a return to intellectual and physical work. From St. Francis to the Little Brothers and Little Sisters of Charles de Foucauld, each new attempt to live in Christ and bring Him to the world has meant a participation in the world of work.

Within the flux of history the Christian aim should be to restore unity and balance to individuals, the Church and society. If the Church has been too otherworldly and scorned the dignity and importance of the Creation, then work and commitment to this world have to be stressed. But on the other hand, when work in this world and work "of this world" has become idolatrous, with progress and productivity the be-all and end-all, then the other facet of truth must be stressed. Besides work in all its levels of meaning, there is also the Christian commitment to rest and contemplation. God worked for six days in the creation story, and on the seventh He entered into His rest. From this Holy Rest came the Sabbath observances and ultimately the Christian idea of contemplative vocations. All is not active struggle and work in its active sense; there is the passive acceptance of plenitude. God will be all in all and the divine mystery must be celebrated in this world by feast, dance, play, and accepting joy. Man made in the image of God must also rest, contemplate and play. Leisure, too, is as important to man and his culture as work.[4] Ironically, in our society and our world Christianity needs to emphasize this protest against utilitarianism, while within the Church there is a need to emphasize the importance of this world and its work. Within the Church there has been too much emphasis upon passivity in this life, too ready an acceptance of suffering, too much reliance upon the supernatural too soon. This world and its work have been viewed too exclusively as cursed and penitential.

In this general concentration upon penance, suffering, and the supernatural world cut off from the natural, women and their work have suffered. Their inferior position in this world and limited work opportunities have been considered of little matter, for in the next world the last will be first, and women, slaves, the poor, etc., would be compensated. Moreover, when the curses of Genesis were overly emphasized, a "woman's work" could be justified. But as I have argued, when theology emphasizes Resurrection and Paradise as the Christian ideal for the here and now, then women, work and sex take on different values. The unity and equality of work that prevailed in Paradise, and prevails among the Resurrected must be lived in present time. Christians must seek to so grow up in Christ that the liberty of the sons of God can be exercised now. In Christ there is neither slave nor free, Jew nor Greek, male nor female—nor is there a special work that each must do. These old divisions are no longer operative or limiting. There is variety and diversity in Christian life and work, but it is a variety and diversity that arises from the diversity of individual vocation, talents and gifts rather than necessity.

The concept of vocations must be renewed along with the modern Church's emphasis upon work. Formerly "vocation" too was limited in application to the religious life . . . to have a vocation meant to be a "religious" (that the term was used so exclusively is also symptomatic). Then, vocation was broadened in popular thinking to include marriage. The married too were called by God to a special and important task in this world: procreation and education of children. The next development is taking place now. Every Christian's vocation extends beyond his specific state and category. An attempt to penetrate to the mystery of the Church in this world has begun, and many of the old juridical and tidy categories are transcended. The Church today returns to Scripture and sees the early Church working as a community with a minimum of hierarchial divisions. Their unity in love and realization of themselves as the people of God was more important than lines of command, states of life and specialization. "Each had his gift" or talents, but these were to be used in concert with others to build up the whole community. The glory and mystery of the body of Christ is that each member developed to his fullest can still be knit into a functioning unity of a whole. With God the giver of every good gift, every good gift can be developed to the full and given back to Him.

Today, as we rethink the meaning of the world, work, and Creation, we realize that non-apostolic work in the world is also a call of God. Man has a vocation to subdue the world, to exercise his sovereignty, to contribute to the New Creation, to develop himself into the new man and to develop the whole created order for God. Frustration, penance, the Cross, will still exist, but Christians fully conscious of the Resurrection will realize that the victory is won though the last battles continue. All work will partake both of victory and battle. There is the exhilarating, creative satisfaction of work as well as the penitential, ascetic side. Both joy and penance are present in work, whether some specific task or the greater work of a whole life.

Each individual life, however, and each vocation is different. The problem is to determine the work God has for the specific person. I have already touched upon this in discussing ways women can come to decisions in planning family life, but essentially, women's problem with work is the same as everyone else's. When there is freedom of choice, and admittedly women's freedom of choice has come late, there is more responsibility before God. Every person is endowed with different gifts, but with each gift and talent there is a corresponding duty to develop it and give it back to God. As in the parable of the talents, the more God has given the more He will require. In this context of gifts, freedom and responsibility, encompassed in the concept of "stewardship," individual conscience and external circumstances determine individual actions. The crux of the matter comes when honest self-assessment impels toward one vocation, while uncontrollable forces impose another work entirely. The Christian must manage the difficult psychological stance of seeking, struggling, striving, and yet suffering defeat patiently in the faith that failure, too, can serve. Everyone must be willing to take up his Cross, but it must be a cross God gives, not a neurotic, passive, or proud retreat or self-denial for itself alone. Since each life is so different and God has a different work for each individual to do, it is almost impossible to determine what is right for another. Certainly some things are wrong for everyone, and some things are wrong for certain people, but in the realm of right and good things there is infinite variety.

There is an infinite variety too for women; for the point must be made again that there is no particular woman's work other than childbearing. Woman and man have the same mission, to increase and multiply and subdue the earth; to restore all things in Christ. Women cannot multiply alone and leave subduing the earth to man; both are responsible

for both commands. Helper and helpmate have been under-
stood for too long in a subordinate sense, and woman considered in her relation to man and his work rather than to
God and God's work. Married woman as a Christian human
being must seek her perfection and vocation in her work as
well as man. Once marriage is chosen as a mutual vocation,
then both are equally responsible for each other and their
children. Childbearing and nursing are woman's unique
privilege and joy, but in our crowded world of today, this
work is a minute portion of a woman's total life-span. The
care and guidance of children, however, takes much longer
than ever before, and in that task mother and father should
share. With this sharing, and the institution of schools, and
work-saving appliances, there will arrive a time in every
woman's life when she will no longer be able to center all
her work energy upon her own home, husband and children.
What then? And long before "then," why are some women
so unhappy in their traditional work? Many, seeing that it is
the educated women who rebel against the traditional role,
decide that it is a case of spoiled women who simply never
grew up. This is certainly true of many who cannot accept
responsibility or the self-giving of the traditional work of
women, but there are also basic principles of satisfying work
at stake.

The first principle, again, concerns individual vocations
within the vocation of marriage. As I have said before, but
must reiterate, marriage today is not a ready-made vocation,
but a state in which two people must turn to their other
work, childrearing and subduing the world in some way. In
this larger dimension of work, individual talents and gifts
and individual work must be adjusted. And the sad fact
which causes all the trouble is that in our culture the traditional role assigned to woman has allowed no flexible adjust-

ment. Everyone has been cast in the same mold regardless of talents. Flexibility of work for different individuals is part of satisfying work. But even more important, work must be necessary and must be done within some community to achieve continuity and meaning. Isolated work without purpose or meaning is pure punishment for man. Frustration for a cause can be borne, penance can be done, but isolated meaninglessness is hell. Although a person can stand work for which he is completely unsuited if it is done in community and serves a good purpose, ultimately the ideal work has communal participation and suits individual workers' capacities and talents.

Throughout most of history men and women have had one part of the ideal by being part of a community as a matter of course. The tribe, the manor, the guild, the clan or family—these communities (reinforced by church and nation) gave men and women a sense of communal life. Besides this, the supernatural community was never very far away, whether in the form of ancestors, spirits, saints, or angels. In comparison, modern man is adrift in a lonely world. Man has always been cruel to man; but isolated meaninglessness has never before been so menacing. One can stand to be isolated if one's universe is intact; or one can see the world as a meaningless thing within a secure community. Neither is as anxiety-producing as being alone with chaos.

The drudgery of past ages was more bearable because of its communal nature, meaning, and obvious necessity. Take, for example, the all-day toil involved in weeding a field. This is satisfying when, one, you know that this is the service God (or the God of fertility) requires of you; two, this toil is necessary for individual and community survival; and three, your family, friends, and peers are working in the field with you. Work-songs, pauses for prayer, food, or water, and perhaps a harvest festival would re-inforce the sense of community life. In an urban context, other occupations before the industrial revolution would also have had built-in certainties of community, guild, cult, culture, and family. In neither country or city were women separated from the larger community while child-bearing or child-rearing. Their work, whatever it might be, included constant interchange with other adults, and was necessary for survival of the family or larger community. Even the unusually isolated pioneer women of the American frontier were performing absolutely necessary work in cooperation with their husbands. They suffered exile from cult, culture and stable community, but they had their husband's company and could never feel that their work had no meaning. The necessity of their labor and its visible results surrounded them.

Many women in our industrial society face far different work situations. Despite the wide variety and disparity of modern women's life-styles, the principles of satisfying work remain the same. Those women who participate in the necessary work of some community which gives meaning to their work are content. If their meaningful work also suits their individual talents, they are very happy. This is basically why some women are content and happy in the traditional role of wife, mother, housekeeper, and culture-bearer, and some are not. Let us take a look at the actual work that may be involved in the traditional role today, and assess its satisfactions and dissatisfactions in relation to meaningfulness and community life.

First of all there is housekeeping, that occupation so maligned and over-glorified. In the maligning department, Betty Friedan asserts that the feeble-minded make good houseworkers and further implies that mere housewifery is only suited for feeble-minded women.[5] She and many another feminist scorn the satisfactions of good housekeeping. They claim that women who are "too good for this," have been sold a bill of goods, and suppressed and tricked into this degrading work. At the other extreme the glorifiers of housekeeping, with both commercial and spiritual variants, claim that complete fulfillment for every woman comes in keeping beautiful houses beautiful, clothes white and bright, and food zestful and nutritious. Somehow such a high standard of aesthetic and material perfection has been set up, that all the women working feverishly all the time with all the new gadgets and products can never win. Sometimes, too, these super-high housekeeping standards are bound up with house-pride and outdoing the neighbors. No wonder that drudging for an impossible goal with the primary motivation being proud display rather than intrinsic value or human use can reduce housekeepers to exhausted unhappiness. If the satisfactions of housekeeping are only in bolstering pride, then the perfect housekeeper (like the Pharisee prominently praying in the front row) has small reward.

But this is not all there is to housekeeping. It can partake of many of the intrinsic satisfactions of other work. Basically the housekeeper is imposing pattern, order and harmony upon diverse components. Out of chaos, confusion, and disorder the houseworker like all other workers struggles to create and maintain unity. Things are scattered, dirtied, torn, broken, rusted, and they must be set right. Food must be planned, gathered, prepared, served, and put away. Appliances must be cleaned, serviced and oiled. In addition, purchases must be decided upon and made, plants and gardens tended, and ornamentation and aesthetic decoration provided. Whether doing diapers, dusting, or devising menus, constant active effort must be expended to keep a house from disintegrating. Organization of effort for a unified purpose is absolutely essential. The feeble-minded person may do housework well, but only if specific tasks are repeatedly assigned. Deciding upon priorities and efficiently unifying effort takes judgment, discipline, and experience. Good housekeeping upon a limited budget takes efficiency, and executive skill as well as physical stamina. Many a modern young woman is overwhelmed by housekeeping, because having seriously underestimated the work she has never been trained in the individual tasks or developed her ability for over-all organization. We could well imitate the Pueblo Indian women who taught their daughters how to first plan the day and then work calmly and steadfastly, to conserve their energy so that every task got done in its proper time and place without strain.

But organization of time and effort is not everything. One level of satisfaction comes from creating and maintaining order, but there is also possible in housework a celebration of the dignity of matter. All of these "things" are a part of the Creation of God; if one is conscious of this truth (or only dimly conscious of it), work with the hands can become even more meaningful. Perhaps Teilhard de Chardin has been the seer who has done most to restore the dignity of matter and work to modern Christian consciousness.[6]

All of creation is waiting for man to master it, while marveling at its mystery. Many housewives know this and find an intrinsic satisfaction in shining, polishing, cleaning, waxing; bringing to perfection and beauty the material object. As for cooking, sewing, decorating, and gardening, they can be even more creatively satisfying since new wholes are created from assorted material objects. If all of these tasks are integrated into the rhythm of the liturgical year, there can be even a greater sense of meaning. Making all things new for the feast of Easter, for example, is appropriate.

At the opposite extreme, the most backbreaking and unpleasant tasks of housekeeping (such as cleaning out the oven or basement) can also give a sense of satisfaction. There can be a penitential offering of such hard work, besides the natural release from self that exhaustion can bring. The aches, pains and blisters of a monumental spring housecleaning are far more satisfying than the nervous fatigue from a day of dissipated ineffectual light housekeeping. All-out physical effort is so necessary to man that every leisure class in history has devised some exhausting sport as a substitute for hard manual labor. The housewives who fear the automation that will make housework obsolete are demonstrating not only their desire to be needed, but the satisfactions of hard work.

Housekeeping has its satisfactions, but they are few compared to the even more important work that must go on in the home: the process of growing together with people. A woman living with her husband and children provides the whole material and mental milieu for personal interchange, or these crucial "inter-personal relations" that shape our mental health. This "work" of growing up with one's family while caring for them is very subtle, indeed. Love makes some things easy, but the inertia of life militates against taking the trouble to really live creatively on all levels. Everyone knows that successful sexual adjustment takes effort and time, but not enough has been said about other growth together which common work and creative conversation can further. Verbal and other communication is as important as the physical language of love for mutual growth. Both partners can grow up together and sanctify one another as they explore and exchange their ideas, emotional reactions, and spiritual ideals. When each develops his or her own initiative with the help of the other, two persons are then working for individual maturity as well as a fuller unity. This mature husband-wife relationship (discussed in Chapter 4) takes constant effort: one does work at marriage.

The woman's work with her children is rather different. Starting from a one-flesh unity, she seeks to develop an independent, mature person who needs her less and less. She works herself out of a job, so to speak. The object is to give so generously and so wisely, that finally one can completely give the child to the world to exercise his own generative powers. The only thing a woman should get from her work at childrearing is her own matured personality and a certain joy in contemplating an independent, developed person. It is right that children grow in wisdom and stature, find their favor with God and man, in order to be able to leave home and mother and go their own way. The family grows up together, indeed, but it does not stay together. A successful job of launching children into their own time of giving requires an understanding of the necessity of detachment in parental love. The times of intense mothering and care (if successful) will gradually grow into a less dependent relationship where guidance and communication is less direct and more subtle. In this work parents learn from their children, for they must widen their own horizons in order to lead and direct. They must intellectually stimulate and convey cultural and religious values. There is intellectual challenge, but this is nothing compared to the moral and emotional demands. Sadly enough, to develop disciplined, happy, loving, good children parents must be self-disciplined, happy, loving, and good themselves. All of the conscious training in the world will fail, if the parents are themselves seriously flawed as people. Intellectual achievement, medical knowledge, even a knowledge of child psychology are as naught if a mother is not mature and loving herself.

But with all the innate satisfactions of homemaking, it, like all work, is most fully satisfying when necessary to a larger community. It is no accident that today's contented homemakers are those who remain in a community much like those characterizing the past. If a woman has a large number of children, and many relatives and friends who live in and out of her house, then homemaking can be more meaningful. The constant company of family and friends gives adult companionship as well as a stronger motivation for all of her housework. If a constant stream of people live in the beautiful house, eat the delicious food, and need the clean clothes to wear, then housekeeping has more personal direct meaning than most kinds of work. It is no longer a lonely isolated effort. The fact of the matter is that some women will groan with laughter at descriptions of the lonely, superfluous housewife. These women can barely cope with the hoardes of people around them, all needing to be fed, clothed and cared for. These "open families" are often ones which practice generous hospitality, taking in the sick, the old, the disturbed, and other people's children who need temporary care. These women do not have to go out to join the community; the community comes to them. Family and community celebrations, meetings for different causes, study groups, religious circles or cell-groups—all gravitate to a generous, hospitable home.

In such a home, the housewife dispenses far more than food and drink. She extends the personal work of the family to others. The homemaker can be a source of wisdom, stimulation, sympathy, judgment, and humor to her whole community. More can go on over endless cups of coffee than gossip and backbiting. I find it ironic that the same people who would praise eighteenth century coffee houses as a positive cultural force, will condemn the merging of coffee and communication when it takes place in a home. Our mass media provide the information and stimulation that one once gathered in the market place, but judgment, balance, and creative thought are only stimulated by conversational exchange of ideas. Intellectual stimulation as well as friendship and love can be the result of small gatherings in the kitchen. Afternoon tea in Bloomsbury or a French salon might possess more aesthetic niceties, but the important result of personal communication anywhere is that hearts and minds meet and grow.

The traditional work of the homemaker, then, consists of a whole spectrum of efforts in different directions. A woman must both manage her house and help herself and her family to mature, as well as minister to those who come her way. Physical effort, emotional effort, intellectual effort—all must be combined into a harmonious whole. Each individual woman lives in different circumstances with different personalities and different problems, so there are no ready-made programs, methods, or routines to follow. Every homemaker must learn to fit the needs of husband, children, house, and herself into her own pattern. The one thing certain is that to do this successfully a person must have personal integrity and wholeness.

Only a developed, mature personality can control and provide a calm center in the whirl and flux of home and family. It takes strength and a secure identity to grasp and mold so many distracting, disconnected elements into a whole. An immature person is simply swept from one crisis to another, overwhelmed by the number and variety of needs and pressures. Only the authentic person essentially inner-directed can successfully manage a work in which she not only decides what her work will include, but must also achieve self-discipline and pressure herself to live up to her own unique standards. Homemaking can be intensely personal, challenging, creative, and most satisfying. The "happy homemakers" are not suffering from delusions.

Most of the happy homemakers are a part of an active social community, but there are two more groups of women who are happy in different ways within the traditional framework. Some women with a developed religious sense, can be so conscious of God's presence and the communion of saints, that they can even suffer the family's physical isolation without harm. Isolated, hard manual labor does not dull them for they remain instant in prayer and spiritually alive. They may be rearing twelve children on a farm away from normal community life, but they can find sufficient sustenance in prayer and the sacraments. Their solitude and constant sacrifices can be borne because they have more than the common measure of the contemplative gift. They can "see the world in a grain of sand," and sense the meaning and mystery of creation behind all the minute, distracting details of daily drudgery. They are soul mates of the Brother Laurence who learned to practice perfectly the presence of God among the pots and pans in his kitchen (admittedly it took him fourteen years!). Such women (and men with similar vocations) imitate the hidden life of Christ, working at physical tasks in communion with God. They serve those few around them with love, and pray for the world and the larger community. Their vocation in the married state is much like that of the contemplative religious.[7] An intense spiritual consciousness can for some transcend the limitations of time and space and the ordinary need of exterior stimulation and support.

Another group of women, often the same women who are spiritually self-sufficient, can perform disciplined intellectual creative work while virtually isolated. The printed word may be their sole intellectual stimulation, but physical isolation for them is simply a welcome solitude in which more serious work is possible. As long as books and journals are available in the home, such women do not require much outside stimulation or pressure in order to work. Their self-discipline is such, that without deadlines, or sometimes without even thought of publication or recognition, a purposeful, disciplined intellectual life is lived. Creative artists can often live in this self-sufficient solitude. In fact, almost anyone whose creative work (determined by some internal necessity) thrives in solitude can lead the full life within the present structure of the traditional woman in the home. After the first rush of baby care is over (it's hard for anyone to do anything else with five children under six), leisure and work schedules can be adjusted so that there is time for personal creative work. The creative woman simply makes time by sacrificing the usual escapist activities. Most women waste enormous amounts of time, so when there is something one wants to do there is always some time to do it. When work is so much a part of a personality, there is no problem in getting it done. The problem is rather getting other obligations attended to; shopping or beauty care can get squeezed out of a busy woman's schedule. Her time becomes so precious that a trip to the beauty parlor inevitably gives way to more important errands. These creative women are so fully stimulated at home (with an occasional trip outside) that as they write, sculpt, paint, etc., they can find the idea of a mere job dull and distracting.

Basically, then, there are three happy groups of women at home: women who enjoy domestic work and do it within a wide communal context, women with a contemplative gift who can participate in a spiritual community, and women with highly creative talents who exercise them at home and participate in the intellectual and artistic community. These groups of women are not immature or degraded because they may not be receiving pay for their work. They would be false to themselves and to their vocations if they were to succumb to a work mystique and to go out and get a job. Their work within the traditional framework is far more meaningful for them and the world, than any job could be. They are happy and can wonder why other women are so dissatisfied.

The dissatisfied women on the other hand are dissatisfied for two very good reasons. (There are also bad reasons for dissatisfactions, selfishness, immaturity, and the like, but they would affect any work anywhere and can be dismissed in this argument.) The justifiable reasons causing dissatisfactions with the traditional work within the traditional structure are (1) that some women are not talented in homemaking, yet it keeps them from exercising their other talents; and (2) whether talented or no, much homemaking today cannot have a meaningful communal context. The first problem of individual talents arises when women do not gain enough stimulation from homemaking and the traditional role. It does not fully challenge certain strong capacities they have. There is, for example, little need at home for continuous, intellectual abstract concentration, nor is there much scope for a highly developed, organizational executive ability, or the kind of creativity that would require, say, an elaborate laboratory. Women with talents in these directions can be very frustrated.

Housekeeping can be a source of frustration too. When prepared foods and ready-made clothes are available, extensive cooking and sewing need only be done for internal creative necessity rather than external economic necessity. And the same is true for furniture refinishing, gardening, decorating, needlework, canning, and other domestic tasks that used to be a necessary part of woman's work. Now, unless a family is very poor, most domestic activities can be streamlined, short-cut or avoided. Fortunately, or unfortunately, the only absolutely necessary domestic skill needed today is efficient organization and management. This lack of external necessity takes the heart out of extensive housekeeping for those who neither enjoy it, do it creatively, or have a sufficiently large group of people needing their work. Many a woman who has been a happy homemaker and not missed other work when challenged by the overwhelming necessities of many pre-school children can find that when her necessary work diminishes, she cannot spend her new-found time upon her housework in order to do it creatively. When confronted with busywork and uncreative frills, then unused talents reassert their demands. Overall frustration can make the lack of continuity in the repetitive non-creative aspect of housekeeping a fatiguing torture. Many women just mark time and half-live endless days longing for the old rushed schedule of young children.

True, women with eighteen children may never face this problem. There is never a time when the necessary direct personal service to others comes to an end (if the grandchildren do not move away, that is). But for various reasons huge families cannot be the solution for most women and their work problems. Besides, having a huge family today is a matter of conscious choice, so that a woman would have to choose to have more children rather than try to find an outlet for her unused talents. When it is a matter of free choice, and most huge families will be deprived families, women are justified in trying to seek the balanced life, in which all of their other talents will be used. This is especially true when the work outside the home she may choose will benefit both her own family and the greater community. The dissatisfied women who as individuals are not fully challenged in homemaking should try for a work life that will more nearly fulfill all their capabilities.

The other great source of dissatisfaction among women is lack of communal context for their homemaking and family life. It must be remembered that many modern women have moved from their birthplace, and will move and move again. On all levels of society families keep going from place to place. Migrant worker or rising executive—both will leave behind parents, grandparents, friends, and relations. And at each destination there is little time to put down roots before another move is at hand. In this situation, no matter how "open" a family may want to be, there is never time for many friendships or for finding those in need or for the community at large to know of their availability. A new family in a community can rarely be a focal point of hospitality or become much of a center of community activity. Whether she chooses to or not, many a woman serves no one beyond husband and children. As a newcomer with small children she can be virtually isolated. The children at least need her, but in the end, her husband becomes her one tenuous link with the adult world and the larger community. Since most husbands cannot adequately live enough for two, the woman's isolation and lack of stimulation can result in a situation that is bad for the family.

Not only does the community not come to the woman in her home, but without help, she cannot get out to the community. Even if a woman can get out, her status as a newcomer keeps her from the most creative and responsible work in the community, be it parish, political party, parent-teacher association, or League of Women Voters. She may have served an adequate apprenticeship in another community, but it takes time in a new place to acquire enough experience to do meaningful community service. Then, in the communities in which the woman finds herself, there may be no volunteer activity which specifically uses her talents and capabilities. No wonder desperation can set in when neither family, homemaking, community activities, or independent creative work in the home fully challenge a woman. What are women to do when barred from viable communities and meaningful individual work?

The answer to this dilemma is the paid occupation outside the home, or, "to go to work." Whether on the level of the job or the privileged plane of the profession, outside work can give women satisfactions that are often unavailable at home. By working many women can avoid busywork, fully challenge otherwise unused potential, and most important, reach the larger community. In uncreative work the money becomes important. If nothing else, money received for services rendered is a sign that someone needs the woman's work enough to pay for it—exit busywork. Money also provides a tangible reward for work and so gives it a meaning, a sense of seriousness and necessity. The money that the woman can contribute to her family can purchase more necessities of life, but also the humane privileges of more privacy, travel, education, and other cultural opportunities. Earning power enables a person to participate in the economic activity of the community, a status that is not to be scorned. Trade and the market-place have been a source of stimulation for every culture; even the despised modern shopping trip is a valid outlet, and sadly enough, sometimes the only communal activity of a family. No matter how uncreative the woman's job, the money she makes can give some minimal status and enlarge her life.

But more important, the job, in addition to providing a sense of being needed and a monetary reward, also provides a disciplined framework and routine. A woman must get up

promptly, do her housework promptly, and above all,
promptly dress to go out. Dress and self-image are so important in American culture that a job which requires a woman
to look attractive and dress carefully, helps her to feel that
she is a worthy person. Reflected in the importance of dress
is the importance of a regular, enforced contact with the
community. Most women need company, and dull work done
with fellow-workers in some communal enterprise is far preferable to too much lonely leisure. There is always some
stimulation in being a part of any group of people, and the
minimal alternation of the different people at home and at
work can provide some variety. Even the change in spatial
surroundings can keep boredom at bay. Work at least gives
you somewhere to go and something to do.

Among the most privileged in the society will be those
women who in their effort to reach out to the community
and fulfill individual talents will not be condemned to dull
work. Their skills and ability can be so used in outside work
that they find their work, in and of itself, one of life's greatest satisfactions. Often, as they impose pattern, order, and
unity in their work, they are also serving the real needs of
others. The continuity, intellectual challenge, creativity, and
contact with the community that they cannot find at home,
they can find at work. Their profession, if zeal, commitment,
and pleasure distinguish a profession from a job, can become
a real vocation in God's service. They love the work for itself
alone, as well as for the psychological and financial rewards.
Only in specialized abstract work are their individual talents
and capabilities fully challenged in a meaningful way in the
larger community. In these cases, the money is secondary.
Arguments proving these working wives do not much benefit
the family economically, thoroughly miss the point. Many a

woman would pay for the privilege of pursuing a profession that for her is stimulating and satisfying.

Most of these women with a drive to work for the value of the work itself are, not surprisingly, the college-educated women. College women are more likely to marry mobile young executives and end up in leisured suburbs far from any stable community of family and friends who need them. Work may be their only avenue to the adult community and their one way of feeling needed. A profession, like a trade or other skills, can travel well. It is, in fact, a guaranteed entree to a like-minded community of colleagues. A continuous commitment to one kind of work is a ready-made outlet for all the excess energy and idealism that one husband, one home and one set of children cannot absorb. In a profession all of one's previous work experience in the field contributes to a growing competence so that through the years continuous work brings a greater effectiveness. An older woman's high level of emotional maturity and a high level of competency will coincide if a woman has been continuously committed and centered her work on certain goals.

College, and the intellectual effort, discipline, and continuity required to earn a degree is but the bare beginning of this commitment. But it is a beginning and enough of a primary model so that it is often in college that a woman will first develop an awareness of both the satisfactions of intellectual work and of her own individual talents. If one has never tasted the joys and satisfactions of continuous arduous, intellectually stimulating work—or if one has never been socially isolated and understimulated—then the dissatisfactions of some women in the traditional role will remain a mystery or a pseudo-problem masking selfishness. Chesterton's famous quote picturing the homemaker as a veritable

Queen Elizabeth deciding all things in her realm is all very well and quite valid, but certainly Chesterton, given a choice, would far rather have written his books. It is doubtful that he would have given up his intellectual work to trade places with Queen Elizabeth herself. The dissatisfied, unhappy homemakers are not suffering delusions, anymore than the happy homemakers. Everything depends upon the correlation of the individuals' capacities to the actual work done, and the meaningfulness and communal context of the work.

A solution, then, should be simple, at least in general outline: to increase the numbers of satisfied women and decrease the numbers of frustrated unhappy ones. But no panacea will work, since it is essentially a matter of individuals or rather individual couples determining a distinct individual pattern and vocation for themselves. The society as a whole, however, can encourage flexible work patterns and diverse models of working women—homemakers, professionals, volunteers, part-time workers—and even perhaps restore the prestige of the leisured lady of culture. With the guiding principle of flexibility for individual vocation and meaningful communal participation, both the traditional realms of women's work and traditionally masculine work could be enlarged. New forms and new flexibility should grace work in the home, church, community, and in jobs and careers.

Let us start with some ideas for the traditional work in the home, the work which most women now do, and which most women in the long run would continue to do. This work, composed of housekeeping and family care, must be granted its intrinsic dignity. Basic housekeeping by itself should be upgraded and apprentice training courses offered to all young people (perhaps during summers). Both men and women should know how to run a house and organize the different activities. Women may have held supremacy in housekeeping recently, but this is one kind of work where men's greater physical strength is clearly an advantage. The major-domo of the past, and the male-staffed housecleaning services of today prove that there is no innately feminine aspect to housekeeping.

As for automation in housekeeping, it should be welcomed and encouraged. Only the most boring repetitive tasks can be automated, anyway. While people should learn how to do tasks without machines (there are children who have never seen dishes washed by hand), when there is a machine that can do the job, then all the better. Teach the people to welcome machines and to spend more time on the more creative tasks which no machine can master. Aesthetic and stylistic values can increase as drudgery decreases. Cooking, gardening, or sewing, for instance, can be (and should be encouraged to be) developed into an art. This art may become a paid occupation, or can benefit the whole community. For example, an expert gardener can get a job or use the flowers from his private gardens to decorate the altar in church or beautify a dreary institution.

The same principle of preparation and community mindedness should hold in the far more important and subtle interpersonal work of the home. Young men and women should be prepared for family life. Instructions, conferences and discussion groups dedicated to bettering marriage and family living should be instituted. There are many such Christian movements already. They should expand and secular counterparts should also be provided. Continuous intellectual and emotional growth should be the family's ideal—individual maturity benefiting family and community. But special emphasis upon preparation for childcare should be given, since all adult lives may be based upon the lessons, consciously and unconsciously learned in childhood. There is really no more important work in the world than child-rearing, yet young men and women embark upon this most responsible task without any knowledge or experience. No teacher or therapist would be allowed to work with children without years of training and study, yet parents who are a thousand times more important receive nothing. An apprenticeship here would also be a blessing. If childrearing were recognized as the important task that it is, and more men and women considered this as a high and noble work, then there might be far more people available for communal childcare needs. How many thousands of institutionalized children need foster homes, and how few families consider opening their homes and using their childrearing skills for others! Not only are more foster families needed, but more institutional parents, counselors, youth workers, and daycare workers.

Of course, the children of the community are not the only ones needing personal care and attention. The old, the sick, and the poor must also be cared for. Every home and every family should turn out to the community and feel responsible to work in some way for the good of all. If women's work in the home could include, as it once did, a more meaningful ministry to those in need, it would be far more satisfying. Convalescence from many an illness (or breakdown) can only be accomplished in some halfway house in which hospitality and individual care and understanding strengthen a person for the world. If only many more families could take on such a work with its direct person-to-person challenge. There is also no reason why the homemakers of each parish could not have a hospitality center in which anyone in the community who was in need could be an honored guest, or even a paying guest for that matter. If mutual love, care, and direct loving service are the marks of the Christian community, there must be some structure for this mutual care upon a local, intimate, community level—a school is not enough.

The Church and its Work is another of the traditional realms in which women's work can grow. Women can participate fully in all of the work of renewal going on in the present. Every structure of the Church from the study of theology to the local altar society can be the opportunity for someone's meaningful work. Every movement, every corner, within the complex whole of the worldwide community, presents different challenges and needs. In postconciliar Christendom, women who form such a large part of the laity, will also have to grow up and show initiative and responsibility. If new apostolic works are needed, or new forms required, women must respond. As the older, paternal, authoritarian attitudes fade, the clergy will realize their responsibilities to the laity, and provide structures through which lay men and women can exercise leadership. Women, as well as men, can be educated to responsibility, and handle authority in a judicious and creative way.

In truth, since there seems to be no intrinsic or valid theological reason against it, there will, I suspect, be women priests eventually. Even more shocking to present-day, orthodox sensibilities would be married women priests, for while some can easily accept the idea of married priests, and some can champion priesthood for women, few can accept both. The acceptance of a Christian equality, sexuality, and freedom now rarely extends so far. Of course, a Church in which dedicated virgins (male and female), and married men and women could all have valid ministries and vocations would be a far differently structured Church. The married priests would probably minister to their immediate neighborhoods, imitating the earliest Christian communities which met in houses, or small, intimate meeting places. Dedicated priests vowed to Christian virginity (still "the better way" because of its greater freedom to love and serve the whole community more perfectly) could serve in neighborhoods too, but also in the cathedrals, the missions, the prisons, the armies, and all the places and situations where family life could be a hindrance rather than a help. Flexibility of individual vocations keyed to communal needs would again be the guiding principle. Woman would not be denied any work in the Church because of her sex alone; if she had a capacity and call to lead, lead she would.

Those who doubt women's innate ability to lead should observe the efficient and creative way many of the secular volunteer organizations of women are run. Within them, women are trained for leadership and acquire the ability to get things accomplished in their community. Women's clubs and organizations have been the butt of much humor, but such unofficial groups are extremely important in a free society and should not be disparaged by feminists who push "jobs" as far better than volunteer work. These volunteer groups of educated, leisured women can provide an organized third force in many a community. In Russia, where all women work, there are no intermediate groups between the individual and the government; there can be no disinterested third force exempt from economic and political control. No organizations of women voters can work for judicial reform of the courts, nor can a women's peace group picket the Kremlin and protest the government's policies. A free

society needs a complex of volunteer organizations as much
as free women need such groups to develop their leadership
as responsible members of the community. Such groups
should flourish as a way of providing meaningful work to
many women. Volunteer work can be the perfect supplement
to homemaking. As the volunteer organizations become more
and more socially conscious and apply themselves to the real
needs of the community, their work will become even more
satisfying for many more women. The volunteer who, for
instance, helps one deprived child in an institution to master
new reading skills over the course of a year, may have much
more satisfaction from her work than from the traditional
fundraising activities of many auxiliary groups. The forgotten people of our society need the concern and interest of
the privileged who will serve without pay.

However, as all women will not find satisfaction in available volunteer activities, whole new structures of education
and work patterns must be devised so that women (and men)
may educate themselves for professional work and pursue it
without harming family life. I repeat the suggestions offered
in the chapter on woman as mother: part-time education,
part-time work, with flexible schedules and family benefits
for men and women. Only with these new structures can
women be assured that their children will have enough parental care and rearing. If women can have the opportunity
to keep studying, to keep growing intellectually, and in some
cases to keep working they and society will benefit.

Nor are these solutions so farfetched. Many free societies
manage some or most of these measures. Institutes provide
guidance and financial help for women seeking part-time
education and employment. Part-time work schedules are
also increasing. Most promising of all are work schedules for

women completely geared to their children's needs: time off
in the summers, time off for special school events in the day,
and a work-day coordinated with the school day or husband's
schedule. All such measures point to the future when flexibility and freedom of work will be available to all, for most
men need more participation in the satisfactions of childrearing, as women need the world of work.

Previous social barriers and social conditioning can be sur-
mounted. If women and society expect more of themselves
and make demands consistent with higher ideals of human
work, progress can be made. After all, child labor and the
eighty-hour week were once considered "necessary" and
"natural."

Christians for their part should lead the way to the good
society and the perfection of man as a worker. The old psychological barriers and conditioned expectations can be transcended by a Christian ability to look at all things from a
totally new viewpoint. Work must be made more human and
all humanity freer to choose meaningful work. Christians
who for centuries have been trained to examine themselves
from a God's-eye view and a Divine standard of perfection
must now extend this view to specific social structures in this
society. Emotional detachment from the "status quo" is the
first step preceding radical revolution and change. A truly
Christian detachment can be the basis for discriminating
judgment and attachment to new measures which will move
this world nearer to the perfect society God demands. Justice, charity, freedom, satisfying work—all these Christian
values must be fulfilled not only within the individual, and
within the Church, but also within the world. *All* things
must be made new, all things restored in Christ; man's work
so central and important to himself and society must be
given new dignity and new satisfactions.

NOTES

[1] Cf. Erich Fromm, *The Sane Society* (New York: Rinehart, 1955).

[2] Brian Wicker, *Culture and Liturgy* (New York: Sheed & Ward, 1963), p. 158.

[3] Dom Rembert Sorg, O.S.B., *Holy Work* (St. Louis: Pio Decimo Press, 1953), p. 119.

[4] Cf. Josef Pieper, *Leisure: The Basis of Culture* (New York: Pantheon, 1952).

[5] Betty Friedan, *The Feminine Mystique* (New York: W. W. Norton, 1963), Chapters 10 and 12.

[6] Cf. Teilhard de Chardin, *The Divine Milieu* (New York: Harper, 1960).

[7] Cf. Solange Hertz, *Women, Words and Wisdom* (Westminster, Md.: Newman, 1959).

SEVEN »»»

Concluding Thoughts for the Future

It would be nice to conclude this book with a simple ringing call for women to do this or that, or follow this or that model of perfect womanhood. Instead, a complex and rather flat conclusion is in order. For the essence of my case is adherence to a balanced ideal which gives freedom to different women to do different things. Variety and uniqueness is a basic principle of human life; different women in different circumstances, with different means, should do different things. Certainly I would argue for personal maturity but also recognize that for different women maturity can mean different things. Some women should follow their traditional vocation as helpmate, homemaker and mother. Other married women should follow their vocations of more independent work in the world beyond the home. With such a non-traditional vocation a woman may be justified in spacing and limiting her family in order to concentrate more time and energy upon her other work in the larger community. But then there need be no rigid correlation between number of children and amount of outside work.

One woman might have three children in order to practice psychiatry while another, happy in a completely traditional role, would also have three. The truth is that individuals vary tremendously in every way, and the stress, strain, rush and confusion which may challenge and stimulate one woman and her family can be very harmful to another. There are even women like the lady who graduated from law school with five children and proceeded to practice law and produce six more; at the other extreme, there are some families which are overwhelmed with two children. The hidden factors in most cases are energy levels, education, economic circumstances, and the family personalities; but a flexible ideal for women and work should include the whole range of possibilities and probabilities. If at this point stress is laid upon the extraordinary women like the lady lawyer or the lady don at Oxford famous for her six children and brilliant philosophical work, it is only to break through the "conditioning curtain" which keeps women who might want to and be able to, from combining the work of the family with other demanding work.

But even when a talented, energetic woman has broken through the expectation barrier, external circumstances can still cause conflicts. It must be emphasized that the individual woman does not exist in a valueless vacuum. Christian women are committed to charity (even to the point of self-sacrifice), indissoluble marriage, and parental childrearing. If conflicts arise between a woman's fulfillment and the good of her marriage, or the welfare of her children, then love may demand self-sacrifice. But then again, not always. The problem becomes more confusing because self-sacrifice too can be wrong. Sometimes and in some cases the right course might well be for husband or children to be forced to become less dependent and make sacrifices of their own for mother's sake. Much depends, naturally, upon the age of the children, the number of children, their personalities, and the circumstances and situation of the family. And since the family not only moves about, but changes composition as members are born, grow up, and leave, the right solution at one moment may not be the right one later. The family is always in a state of flux, and the parents who must direct and guide the development while being a part of it themselves, must have a true insight into the situation of everyone concerned in order to make the right decisions.

St. Ignatius termed this important faculty of insight "discernment of spirits," a good name for the subtle art of analyzing and judging persons and particular situations. Men and women want to do what God wills for them, but in order to do so they must first understand themselves and their own situation. They must also have faith that if they seek, they shall find. The Christian may be initially puzzled about what he should do, but if he has prayed, sought human advice, meditated, and prayed again, he most probably can discern what is right for him to do—a continuing martyrdom of agonized uncertainty is rare.

Indeed, a measure of peace, tranquillity, and the happiness of the person is a sign and argument that he or she is doing what God wants. That is (according again to St. Ignatius[1]) if the person is generally going toward God and seeking Him. If the person is instead running away from God, then wrong actions cause the illusion of peace; and the effort to turn again and repent may cause unhappiness. Generally speaking, however, our inner peace and contentment are a sign of right thought and action, a guide for finding our vocation. Happiness must be the norm, and the agonizing sacrifice (that does not bring mental peace, at least) should be the exception.

As everyone knows, there is suffering and suffering. An isolated missionary can suffer every mental and physical hardship and still be content, even joyful. And this situation parallels the plight of many mothers. Sacrifice and suffering mastered can be redemptive for the individual and the community. Such sacrifices can be freely chosen. But the suffering involved in mental illness or the personality breakdown of brainwashing could never be freely chosen. Such overwhelming suffering should be resisted for it involves the destruction of the personality, the self and the identity created by God to know Him and love Him. Like the suffering of those who do evil, the suffering of personality destruction is diabolic. God desires "free sons of God" who have "grown up into Christ," not crushed automatons without freedom, without identity, who in the end are incapable of "taking up" their cross. Unfortunately, some women in the past have made too many of the wrong sacrifices; they have been guilty of a suicide of personality.

For too long Christians and Christian women have confused free sacrifice, service, and obedience with passivity, servility, and self-destructive acquiescence. The present crisis of women's role in the Church and world, is related to the larger problems of Christian vocation, freedom, obedience and authority. All such problems cannot be solved overnight, but the basic prerequisite is a new understanding of the initiative and personal responsibility of the Christian, both within the Church and without in the world. When Father Rahner condemns the last centuries of Christianity as too "feminine," he is condemning a passive acquiescence to tradition and authority. Such a servile ideal of obedience spawned the fatal inertia exemplified by German Catholics toward Hitler. It is a terrible indictment of women and traditional femininity when "feminine" is an adjective describing basic immaturity. If I cannot conclude with ringing calls for specific action, I can at least manage some indignant denunciations of the inadequacy and harmfulness of previous ideas about woman's nature and work.

The feminists are right in this: attitudes toward woman in the past have encouraged injustices, irresponsibility, neurotic withdrawals, and stunted personalities in untold numbers. The unfair system (like slavery) may have encouraged unsung saints, but this fact does not excuse it. Christians want more than a "fair-unfair" morality, but justice is the minimum requirement; only then can most men flourish and the few freely choose sacrifice beyond the law. The pagan emphasis upon the difference of the sexes, and woman's confinement to passive, submissive roles harmed family life and society as a whole. Legal, social, and educational limitations —all basically unjust and unchristian—have been rationalized by bad theology, a false mystique of sacrifice, and misunderstandings of biological determinism. Furthermore, the subjugation of women has been part and parcel of a wrong Christian attitude toward this world and the flesh, and at the same time, a too materialistic emphasis upon the biological and physical. Unfortunately, agnostic otherworldliness and materialistic glorification of sexuality have joined forces to condition women to submit and accept unnecessary limitations.

The bad theology of woman was based on bad scriptural exegesis. But perhaps these interpretations of Scripture which furthered feminine suppression were more misguided than culpable. In the patriarchal context of the ancient world, with its misunderstandings of biology, it was only natural that the New Testament's message of woman's new freedom in Christ was gradually obscured by the minor theme of their seemly and traditional subordination under the Law. The negative and ambiguous texts (like those referring to slaves) were read out of context and used to buttress the existing culture's masculine privilege and authority. Perhaps without modern biblical scholarship, and certainly without the renewal of theology, Eve and women would still be labelled the gateway to sin.

The cult of Mary as the New Eve was no real remedy for discrimination against woman. The glorification of Mary and the eternal feminine still emphasized spiritual differences between the sexes which again justified the subordination of women to man as heart to head, intuition to reason, passivity to action. Only as Eve, Mary, and the rest of women regain their primary identity as human beings related to God and the whole human community, can a Christian ideal of woman be restored. Women and men are made first for God and then for each other and the world. Woman's primary end is Christ, and her primary obligation to do God's will; "in Christ there is neither . . . male nor female." The revelation of feminine equality and freedom which Genesis pictured is fulfilled in Christ.

The patriarchal family can be compared with the Law: both served a real purpose in the past. A paternal, hierarchical family organization is far better than complete anarchy, and it does insure (by the bribery of power perhaps) male responsibility for wife and children. However, in the fullness of time, when mature Christian men and women voluntarily assume full family responsibilities, Christian unity, charity, and liberty supersede patriarchy. When the married couple can achieve a one-flesh unity of equality "as it was in the beginning," then both members can look to Christ, the Church, and each other, for guidance rather than to masculine authority. In a Christian scheme of values, the husband's masculine privilege is as outmoded as the privilege and authority of the eldest son over his younger brothers.

Patriarchy and primogeniture with their inevitable injustices may once have been worth their cultural price, but they are no more.

Hopefully, Christianity will see our Western manifestation of the patriarchal society wither away just as transmuted and secularized Christian values obviated slavery and the rigid feudal caste system. The secular movement for the emancipation of women is as basically Christian as the Revolutionary cry for Liberty, Equality, Fraternity; and quite naturally it will repel all those committed to the status quo. If conservatives during the French Revolution could point with horror to the Terror, modern conservatives on the woman question can decry divorce, neglected children, the death of loving sacrifice, and the many aggressive, selfish and shrewish modern women. True, many good things are now being slighted in our changing society. But they do not have to be. Christians can, for once, lead the way to a new synthesis of values by welcoming the changes and formulating an ideal which incorporates all the worthwhile older values along with the new. The present turmoil can be an opportunity to substitute more Christian values where before there existed indifferent but enshrined patriarchal customs and concessions to outgrown economic and biological necessities.

A new Christian synthesis should welcome the new emphasis upon the individual woman's fulfilling herself as a person, and at the same time emphasize community and the importance of woman's work and commitment to the family and home. The new synthesis could stress the range of personal creativity and satisfaction available in the home, family, and volunteer work, as well as recognize creative commitments to professional work and the satisfactions of paid employment.

Above all, a new Christian synthesis would welcome a

wider range of acceptable modes and patterns for marriage. Various combinations of childrearing and outside work will further individual freedom and flexibility of development. Instead of stringent sexual stereotypes and rigid cultural patterns, there can be a more complete and demanding standard for the mature human person whether male or female. To achieve this there need be no confusion of sexual identity or a downgrading of procreation, but more of a recognition that sexual identity, sexual activity, and procreation itself are a base upon which the person and family build rather than an ultimate value. In the same way an individual's work would be important as it contributed to his development as a person, but neither work nor sex in themselves can be a substitute for personal identity, meaningful community, or lasting goals. The human person and human society may not be able to develop without the functions of sex and work, but the total person and the world have a reality beyond these partial realities.

While sexuality and work are rightly valued as a means to reach other people and other things (a pale imitation of the divine creativity), still they remain only a means. The means of participating in community cannot be more important than the individual and the communal goal. A mystique of work or a sexual mystique will always fail the human being, for ultimately the human being must primarily "be." Each person must be capable of standing alone before he or she can give or benefit from communion with others. Christians who believe that God has given them being and that communion with Him is the ultimate goal, will always resist substitute religions. Neither femininity, family life, or work, or a combination of these can finally satisfy women. Work as a rationale for life is particularly fragile, too easily destroyed by old age, retirement, sickness, or unemployment. When work and the flesh and family all fail, *then* the test of human resources and values begins. The trouble with work and sexual substitutes for religion is that they can only function for the elite few at a favored time of life, i.e. the talented, attractive, intelligent, educated, and economically privileged, during their healthy adulthood. Unfortunately, the whole truth of human experience includes failure, evil, suffering, and death. I have called this recognition of objective limitations a reality principle for women; for some women will simply never have a chance to achieve any of their ideals.

Not that the recognition of evil or the limitations of present reality excuses any one from struggle; if nothing else, present efforts can change the culture for the next generation. The crucial time to initiate change is, of course, in the formative years. If we want women and men and society to be different from the past, then we must not only try to be different ourselves but raise our children differently. Legislated emancipation, such as the right to vote, will do no group any good if they and their culture do not change concurrently. Family life is crucial to this change.

It has become evident that at the very beginning of a human life sexual prejudice can make a difference. Parents who do not overcome strong preferences for one sex or another during pregnancy can harm their children. There may be a delight in variety when the first boy or girl arrives in a family, but there should never be any disappointment that a baby was not of the opposite sex. The realization that every baby is a unique human person, a creation of God destined for eternal life, outweighs the importance of sexual identity. From the moment of birth, the sex of the child must be completely accepted and never regretted. Before sexual identity can be transcended in the Christian life, it must first be securely grasped by the small child; his parents' joyful acceptance is the first necessary condition in securing a basic self-acceptance. A primary identification with the parent of the same sex can be more easily effected if the parent is loving and spends time with the child.

Moreover, distinctive masculine and feminine dress and hairstyles can help this initial identification process, just as individual clothes can help a person to a sense of personal identity. Certain masculine sports can be taught small boys and played with fathers; while little girls should be near pregnant and nursing mothers. Naturally both sexes should be instructed about the facts of life, but girls should know of the joys of feeling the baby within, the wonder of childbirth, and the pleasures of nursing. When the feminine role in procreation is felt to be a privilege, then menstruation can be the proud sign of maturity. Physical development, health, and bodily strength should be encouraged in girls so that they can carry well and have the stamina to care for their children. Ironically, in our culture with less heavy laboring work for men, women need to be the stronger. If many a woman could have had the physical training of her brothers (perhaps concentrating on back muscles and general endurance), the destructive fatigue of pregnancy and childrearing could be lessened. A mother's energy and health is so basic in family life, that every young girl should develop physical fitness through exercise and sports.

Preparation for family life should also be the theme and goal guiding children's sexual education. Children should be taught that sexual expression is a good and pleasurable mode of conveying a couple's love, unity, and life commitment, a unity which may be blessed by the creation of a child. When the serious context is recognized and the total commitment secure, then the pleasure and the playfulness of sex can flourish. Only the idea of sex as a light game one wins or loses should be anathema. The realization of each person's unique value and worth must automatically make any use of another person reprehensible. Here, the primacy of human identity over sexual identity can guard against using sexual prowess for personal popularity, selfish pleasure, or economic security.

It must also be very clear that the dreadful double standard is a pagan practice; Christians and a Christian society demand a single high standard of personal morality in which word and deed, coitus and commitment correspond absolutely. Only then can marriage become the cooperative work of two loving and equal persons and never a mutual exploitation. Adolescents must be imbued with the idea that each partner in a marriage is responsible for the perfection and development of himself, his partner, and the family as a whole. At this point in our society the man's temptation is to desire an ego-inflating subordinate, while women often long for a father substitute who will take care of them. In the struggle for maturity it is as hard to give up hereditary privilege as it is to take initiative and new responsibilities.

Maturity can only come when the sexes accept each other as similar and equal, and demand the same personality goals and work performances. Girls should be expected to show as much initiative, curiosity, and responsibility for the world as boys; boys would be expected to be as cultivated and sensitive as girls, and as devout. The hard, ruthless, insensitive man would be as repugnant as the aggressive woman is today. Inevitably, an openness and concern for others imposes courtesy and self-restraint; the result is gentle-men and gentle-women. Faults and transgressions cannot be lightly excused as typical masculine or feminine failings. Boys cannot be allowed aggression and violent destruction, nor girls a charming deceitfulness. The complete human ideal demands

early formation in a single standard of morality. Christ is the
reference point of perfection rather than custom and culture.
Girls in particular must be raised to serve God and their
neighbor rather than to please and attract men. A young girl
must give primacy to finding her meaning as a mature person
in relation to God and the world, rather than concentrating
upon her relationship to men. She must first develop herself
and her capacities.

In an effort to help both boys and girls to develop into
complete persons, toys, social opportunities, expectations,
and education should not be sex-limited or sex-linked. Beyond reproduction and some sports, good activity or interest
should never be discouraged because it is not masculine or
feminine. Girls should certainly be given dolls, but boys
should not be discouraged from playing with them. Boys
should develop their talents for babycare and be competent
in housework. Girls should not only be encouraged to master
housekeeping skills, but also develop interests in outdoor activities, intellectual pursuits, and science. Preconceived no-
tions of what kinds of work men and women do should not
influence a parent to influence a child. Girls especially need
to be exposed to women who do all sorts of work, and boys
need to meet men who are artists, or teachers, or dancers.
Individual talent and individual vocation is a better guiding
principle than rigid cultural concepts of what men do, and
women do.

Formal education should also emphasize the openness and
wide range of opportunity for the individual regardless of
sex. In fact, girls should be forced to take mathematics and
science and boys to take history of art. After required subjects have exposed the students to many sides of the intellectual spectrum, then they can more aptly gauge their own
capacities and interests. When intelligent, seriously com-

mitted girls are not socially penalized or forced to choose
between family and serious work, then more girls will go on;
they will have somewhere to go. Hopefully, early marriages
will diminish when the pressure toward but one kind of success for women is lessened. Religious vocations too should
increase (if the feminine orders keep to their course of
"aggiornamento").

Within marriage, the control of fertility will make couples
more responsible for the number and spacing of children.
The spectre of overpopulation, even in the West, makes it
likely that small families may one day serve the common
good. Having children will be a greater privilege than ever,
but the smaller family will increase women's responsibilities
to the larger human family. Each woman must be prepared
to serve the larger community, in her own particular way
and work. Undoubtedly, there will be increasing numbers
of women who work outside the home almost continuously.
This will be a good development *if* flexible scheduling and
father's family participation insure parental childrearing; for
Christians are committed to rearing their own children with
but a minimal of substitution of home and family.

Yet, as serious intellectual work is more and more thought
of as feminine, even women in the traditional role will
be willing to cultivate the intellectual life at home. Father
Antonin Sertillanges states in *The Intellectual Life*[2] that
serious intellectual work can be undertaken with but two
concentrated hours a day. Only self-discipline, organization,
and sacrifice of other distractions make such work possible,
but the rewards are tremendously satisfying. Many creative
people have worked no more than two hours a day; Virginia
Woolf, for instance, wrote but two hours every day (standing
up to insure absolute alertness). Most women at home could
manage two hours, but alumnae surveys of college graduates'

reading provide gruesome proof that while modern women may keep their figures, they let their minds go to seed. Women as a minimum discipline should never allow themselves to read at a lower level than the highest level of comprehension they once attained. Former college women may not be reading much when swamped with babies, but what they do read should be stimulating their mind, not anesthetizing it.

If a college education has been truly successful, the years at home with small children can be a time of intellectual growth. All the things one could not get to read in the race for a degree, or in the rush of working can be thoroughly pursued. If a woman plans to go back to work or school eventually, the years when young children and straitened budgets keep a woman at home can become an extensive reading period, a time for study and broadening horizons.

The two most basic aims of the woman-at-home's reading will be consolidation and exploration of new fields. Often, filling in the gaps of one's education can result in pure pleasure. Since the classic works of literature are increasingly ignored in modern education, a treasury of delight awaits the newly released reader. Orgies of reading can be justified when most of the day is given over to the arduous manual labor of early childcare. Plays, poetry, all of Dickens, all of Trollope, even the indulgence of (good) historical novels will not seem a surfeit of sweets when other pleasures have receded beyond the diaper pail. All the intellectual journals one can afford can be swallowed whole and indiscriminately during coffee breaks. Every source of intellectual stimulation must be received as the desert dweller welcomes rain.

Eventually, however, family pressures lessen and a more disciplined pattern of reading develops in which certain aims and goals replace chance selection. The fight for intellectual survival through use of the pleasure motivation recedes. One begins to explore new areas of knowledge in depth and concentrate upon certain problems. While individual vocation and individual circumstances determine selectivity, such fields as childcare, education, theology, and government are pertinent to every woman in every community. The transition from passivity to active purposeful study is natural. The Renaissance man developed in many different directions, but he *developed* through disciplined active response to his studies. When he studied music, he composed; when learning Greek and Latin, he translated; with poetry he composed sonnets. Obviously, the busy housewife without a "room of her own" may only succeed in having a desk of her own with little quiet, or even but a notebook of her own. However, any active efforts to impose form and pattern upon one's reading are worthwhile; continuity checks chaos and the merest shred of creative effort stimulates more creativity. Many women as they grow intellectually find that their real interests are different from the field in which they originally sought training.

Men, too, develop and change their interests, but they are often trapped by the economic pressure to support a family. Women, when and if they do emerge into the world, can truly know who they are and what they want to do. The absence of economic and social pressure can be a hindrance to self-development in many ways, but it can also be a blessing. Leisure, wide general reading, and, above all, the experience of the concrete realities of family and community life can radically change a person's perspective. The widely held opinion of women's innate wisdom, compassion and idealism may really be but the result of their experience in the family and their greater isolation from the competitive struggle for success. A recognition of the advantages of "growing time" motivates the recommendations that students take several years out in work experience (be it in job, slum, or Peace Corps) before completing the long grind of professional training.

Many women today could well stop complaining and meditate upon the truth that only she who is faithful over a little will be faithful over much. Those who rule well do so because they too went through their novitiate. The world needs mature, unpampered persons who bring an inner stability with them, those persons who can cope with anything because they know how to give of themselves. Family life provides this challenge; girls become women in the early difficult years, or they never grow up at all. But men also need family life to grow up. The passing of patriarchy is in my mind a Christian development that will benefit men as much as it frees women. Mutual equality, freedom, and responsibility will strengthen family life and develop more mature Christians.

The traditional division of work may still hold, but it should be a family pattern freely chosen by both partners. In addition, other patterns of dividing family and community or professional work should also flourish; individual vocations, family needs and community needs may be balanced differently in different families. There is no reason why a complex and sophisticated culture cannot affirm many different vocation patterns, and divisions of work. The satisfactions and dignity of housekeeping and homemaking can be affirmed along with those of professional work. The culture can acknowledge the primary importance of childrearing and family life as well as the values inherent in intensive dedication to the larger community of world and Church.

The Christian vision of community has always been one of unity from diversity with a variety of vocations, and gifts contributing to the common good. The free service of many different individuals is knit together in charity. Now that mankind possesses new economic and scientific knowledge, marriage can more perfectly imitate the larger Christian community with a variety of vocations and works. Today, many married women can respond to their responsibility for family, Church, and world in many new and different ways. Truly the woman who grows up into Christ faces many new and disturbing challenges of Christian freedom and charity. But in the end, who would willingly retreat?

NOTES

[1] Cf. John D. Gerken, S.J., *Toward a Theology of the Layman* (New York: Herder & Herder, 1963), pp. 122-152.

[2] A. G. Sertillanges, O.P., *The Intellectual Life* (Westminster, Md.: Newman, 1948).